God's Problem

Charlene J. Johnson

Love Clones Publishing
www.lcpublishing.net

God's Problem
Copyright @ 2014 by Charlene Joy Johnson

All rights reserved. No part of this book may be reproduced, stored in a retrieval system, or transmitted in any form or by any means – electronic, mechanical, photocopy, recording, scanning, or any other, without the prior written permission of the publisher.

Scripture quotations marked "KJV" are taken from the Holy Bible, King James Version (Public Domain)

Scripture quotations marked (NLT) are taken from the Holy Bible, New Living Translation, copyright © 1996, 2004, 2007 by Tyndale House Foundation. Used by permission of Tyndale House Publishers, Inc., Carol Stream, Illinois 60188.
All rights reserved.
http://www.newlivingtranslation.com/
http://www.tyndale.com

The Reese Chronological Bible
Authors Edward Reese, Frank R. Klassen
Publisher: Bethany House Publishers, 1980

ISBN: 978-0692307670

Love Clones Publishing
Chicago, IL
www.lcpublishing.netm

DEDICATION

To my late parents Hampton & Beatrice L. Johnson who loved me enough to shape my character with godly principles. Also to my three pastors who represent the stages of my growth in the Lord to bring me to this point in my journey: Pastor Emeritus William J. Vance, the late Pastor James E. Watson and my current Pastor Donald C. Luster, Sr.

TABLE OF CONTENTS

FOREWARD..7

Part I: God Had A Problem............................12

Part II: Jesus' Problem..................................38

Part III: God's Last Problem.........................105

FOREWORD

Minister Charlene Joy Johnson is a woman of God in every sense of "The Word." When I say "The Word," I mean in every sense of The Word of God. This book is a testament to her faithfulness and love for Christ who is her Lord and Savior.

Minister Charlene is an evangelist, teacher, mentor, and intercessor in the highest ranks of warfare prayer. Minister Joy is a spring of truth, integrity, and power of the Holy Ghost. Minister Johnson is a trustworthy leader, faithful servant and reliable friend fit and ready to take the message of the Gospel to the uttermost ends of the earth, which she has already done.

Serving in ministry is a call she embraced with passion because she knows the depth of the love God has for souls. When the Lord put on her heart to teach the world about the nature and character of God she began to pray. She is careful to hear the words of the Lord and record this heartfelt message to whosoever will hear and receive Him.

These are the reasons that Minister Charlene Joy Johnson has written this book, and why she is qualified to speak this word from God to you. I am writing this foreword because I am qualified to speak to the validity that she practices what she teaches you in this book in her ministry. Because of her teaching me what you will learn in the pages of this book I'm a soul saved since 1973, filled with the Holy Ghost, set apart unto Christ. Thanks be unto God who first loved us for using Minister Charlene Joy Johnson as a hand to reach out to the lost.

Christ's Servant,
Lorraine Render
Executive Producer
Lorraine Render Productions

FOREWORD

Rev. Charlene "JOY" is one of God's special gifts to His Church. She excels in didactic and expository, rather than hortatory gifts. In an age when the Church generally has learned to approach the Word of God lightly she has a refreshingly sane influence, reminding humanity of the fundamental facts upon which the Faith is based. She feels more than ever the difficulty and responsibility of a task which is well worthy to occupy the whole time and strenghth of life, and which carries in it its own rich reward.

God's Problem was written from the original sources of friend and foe, in the spirit of truth and love, "sine ira et studio", "with malice towards none, and charity for all," in a clear, fresh, plain style, under the guidance of the twin parables of the mustard seed and leaven, as a book of life for instruction, correction, encouragement, as the best exposition and vidication for the children of God. It is the pedagogy of instruction and immutable facts, of authority and telling, and of right and wrong answers.

In writing this book God's Problem, the aim was to achieve a simple, readable text which would ring true to those who are already lovers of the Gospel of Jesus Christ and would attract others to it. I express my deep appreciation to my friend, my co-laborer and my sister, Rev. Charlene "JOY" Johnson, a scholar of rare learning and microscopic accuracy, for her sincere and valuable contribution to the body of Christ.

Rev. Johnson's intellect is massive without being heavy. She is a most delightful colleague with a sincere and pure heart for God. Like many who have dwelt in close communion with their Lord, she is full of fun and gracious humor. Her presence is always a benediction.

It is in every way fitting, and I am sure will be profitable to many, that this little book of studies has been now given to the Church. No words of any of us are needed to commend a book by Rev Charlene "JOY" Johnson to the body of Christ. God's Problem is an exposition of God's Providence, God's Plan, God's Purpose and God's Provision.

I feel deeply honored and priviledged by having been asked to write this little "Foreword." I pray that in this book God will be glorified, the readers edified, the children of God sanctified, the saints of God unified and every demon in hell terrified.

Rev Donald C. Luster Sr.
MCPM, CMBA, MCCM

PART I
GOD HAD A PROBLEM

God had a Problem:

After God had completed His perfect world He wanted someone to enjoy and appreciate what He had made. So the Godhead: God the Father, God the Word and God the Holy Ghost, decided to make a very unique being, one like themselves that had never existed before.

> *Genesis 1:26: And God said, Let us make man in our image, after our likeness: and let them have dominion over the fish of the sea, and over the fowl of the air, and over the cattle, and over all the earth, and over every creeping thing that creepeth upon the earth.*

God placed His man in a section of His creation called the Garden of Eden on the planet Earth. There the man had full liberty to care for the garden and be nourished by its many wonderful and delicious fruits, vegetables and herbs. There was only one tree in the entire garden from which the man could not eat. In the midst of the garden stood the tree of the knowledge of good and evil. God told Adam this tree was deadly; if he ate its fruit he would die.

> *Genesis 2:16-17: And the Lord God commanded the man, saying, Of every tree of the garden thou mayest freely eat: [17] But of the tree of the knowledge of good and evil, thou shalt not eat of it: for in the day that thou eatest thereof thou shalt surely die.*

God had created the entire universe and said it was all, good. When He created Adam He called it very good; very good because Adam was made in His own image. God had made His man like Himself.

Everything was wonderful in the garden. God and His man enjoyed each other's company and the beauty of God's creation every day. Things were really going great, until God noticed His man becoming more and more curious about the one tree with its forbidden fruit.

> *Genesis 2:18: And the Lord God said, It is not good that the man should be alone; I will make him an help meet for him.*

What was going on in Adam's mind that made God say it was not good for the man to be alone? Perhaps Adam had questions: What will happen if I touch the tree and its forbidden fruit? What is evil? What will happen if I eat this fruit? What does it mean to die?

God decided His man needed help. So God put Adam to sleep and pulled out of him all the parts he needed to fashion into the helper called woman. God made the woman his wife and Adam named her Eve.

> *Genesis 2:21-23 And the Lord God caused a deep sleep to fall upon Adam and he slept: and he took one of his*

> *ribs, and closed up the flesh instead thereof; [22] And the rib, which the Lord God had taken from man, made he a woman, and brought her unto the man. [23] And Adam said, This is now bone of my bones, and flesh of my flesh: she shall be called Woman, because she was taken out of Man.*
>
> *Genesis 3:20: And Adam called his wife's name Eve; because she was the mother of all living.*

When Adam showed his new wife their surroundings he was very proud of the position God had given him over the whole creation. But when they came to that beautiful tree in the garden, called "the tree of the Knowledge of Good and Evil," Adam told Eve the fruit of this tree could not be eaten. He said if you even touch that tree you'll die. Eve nodded in agreement but she didn't really understand. After all – What did it mean to die, anyway?

Adam and Eve's curiosity continued to grow. They began to spend more and more time hanging around the untouchable tree and pondering its meaning.

One day God's enemy, Lucifer, used a creature in the garden to talk to Eve about the untouchable tree. Lucifer began as an anointed angel created by God. Lucifer was beautiful he got caught up in his own glory and thought he could usurp God's authority and become the ruler of the Kingdom

God has created.

The problem was Lucifer had no glory of his own. Lucifer was noting without the presence of God upon him. When Lucifer and his followers rebelled against God they were expelled from heaven and condemned to eternal separation from God and the glory they once knew. As a result they set themselves to destroy God's people and all creation by any means necessary until the day they face their final judgment. *(Isaiah 14:12-15, Ezekiel 28:13-19 & Revelation 12:7-10)*

As the serpent began to talk to Eve, it caused her to doubt the warning she had been given by her husband who was there listening. Eve reached up and touched the fruit – nothing happened. She plucked the fruit – nothing happened. She bit and ate the fruit, still – nothing happened! She gave the fruit to Adam who had watched the whole thing. He took the fruit – nothing happened. He ate the fruit – everything changed!

Adam and Eve realized they were exposed and naked. They tried to cover themselves and hide from God. They knew something had gone really wrong.

Genesis 3:6-8: And when the woman saw that the tree was good for food, and that it was pleasant to the eyes, and a tree to be desired to make one wise, she took of the fruit thereof, and did eat, and gave also unto her husband with her; and he did eat. [7] And the eyes of them both were opened, and they knew that they were naked; and they sewed fig leaves together, and made themselves aprons. [8] And they heard the voice of the Lord God walking in the garden in the cool of the day: and Adam and his wife hid themselves from the presence of the Lord God amongst the trees of the garden.

Now God has a problem. His man was no longer the man He had created in His own image. Adam had disobeyed God's command and was no longer in the image of the Eternal God. He had separated himself from God and become subject to death. God's man had set in motion the course of death and now the whole creation is infected with death due to the disobedience of one man.

Romans 5:12 (KJV): Wherefore, as by one man sin entered into the world, and death by sin; and so death passed upon all men, for that all have sinned:

The all powerful, all knowing, everywhere present at the same time, never changing, only wise God had created everything out of Himself by the Word of His power. To whom would a God like that take His problem? Himself!

Genesis 1:1: In the beginning God created the heaven and the earth.

John 1:1: In the beginning was the Word, and the Word was with God, and the Word was God.

Hebrews 1:1-3: God, who at sundry times and in divers manners spake in time past unto the fathers by the prophets, [2] Hath in these last days spoken unto us by his Son, whom he hath appointed heir of all things, by whom also he made the worlds; [3] Who being the brightness of his glory, and the express image of his person, and upholding all things by the word of his power, when he had by himself purged our sins, sat down on the right hand of the Majesty on high;

God had the Solution:

Adam had disobeyed God's command. He did exactly what God told him not to do. The consequence of this act was what God called death. This condition separates one from God and eventually from this natural world. To go against God's command is the same as breaking God's law. What Adam did, God calls sin. God says sin causes death.

> *Romans 6:23: For the wages of sin is death …*

The process that caused Adam to sin is known as temptation. Temptation came when Adam's desire was opposed to God's command.

> *James 1:13-15: Let no man say when he is tempted, I am tempted of God: for God cannot be tempted with evil, neither tempteth he any man: [14] But every man is tempted, when he is drawn away of his own lust, and enticed. [15] Then when lust hath conceived, it bringeth forth sin: and sin, when it is finished, bringeth forth death.*

The penalty for sin would have to be paid. Someone would have to die. The remedy for death would have to be found. According to God's own word, if a man would keep all of God's laws and live without sinning, death would have no right to claim him. And this man's blood would contain the antidote for death.

Leviticus 18:5: Ye shall therefore keep my statutes, and my judgments: which if a man do, he shall live in them: I am the Lord.

Galatians 3:12: And the law is not of faith: but, The man that doeth them shall live in them.

Leviticus 17:11: For the life of the flesh is in the blood: and I have given it to you upon the altar to make an atonement for your souls: for it is the blood that maketh an atonement for the soul.

God had a New Problem:

Where to find a sinless man? God began to search the annals of time:

NOAH lived in a time when man's wickedness was so great God couldn't stand it anymore. He decided to destroy all human life by flooding the earth. God saved only Noah and his family because He found Noah to be a just man. But Noah wasn't sinless. He wouldn't do.

Genesis 6:8-9: But Noah found grace in the eyes of the Lord. [9] These are the generations of Noah: Noah was a just man and perfect in his generations, and Noah walked with God.

Genesis 6:22: Thus did Noah; according to all that God commanded him, so did he.

JOB was an honest and upright man who reverenced God and hated evil. But Job wasn't sinless. He wouldn't do.

> *Job 1:1: There was a man in the land of Uz, whose name was Job; and that man was perfect and upright, and one that feared God, and eschewed evil.*

ABRAHAM was in right standing with God because he believed what God told him. But Abraham wasn't sinless. He wouldn't do.

> *Romans 4:3: For what saith the scripture? Abraham believed God, and it was counted unto him for righteousness.*

ISAAC was the son God had promised to Abraham. Born in his old age when he and Sarah, his wife, were well beyond their child-bearing years. But Isaac wasn't sinless. He wouldn't do.

> *Genesis 21:1-3: And the Lord visited Sarah as he had said, and the Lord did unto Sarah as he had spoken. [2] For Sarah conceived, and bare Abraham a son in his old age, at the set time of which God had spoken to him. [3] And Abraham called the name of his son that was born unto him, whom Sarah bare to him, Isaac.*

JACOB was the chosen twin. His name was changed to Israel because he would father a nation. But, Jacob wasn't sinless. He wouldn't do.

Genesis 25:28: And Isaac loved Esau, because he did eat of his venison: but Rebekah loved Jacob.

Genesis 35:10: And God said unto him, Thy name is Jacob: thy name shall not be called any more Jacob, but Israel shall be thy name: and he called his name Israel.

JOSEPH was the favored son of Jacob and his beloved Rachel. He provided for his people during a worldwide famine. But, Joseph wasn't sinless. He wouldn't do.

Genesis 30:22-24: And God remembered Rachel, and God hearkened to her, and opened her womb. [23] And she conceived, and bare a son; and said, God hath taken away my reproach: [24] And she called his name Joseph; and said, The Lord shall add to me another son.

Genesis 45:6-7: For these two years hath the famine been in the land: and yet there are five years, in the which there shall neither be earing nor harvest. [7] And God sent me before you to preserve you a posterity in the earth, and to save your lives by a great deliverance.

MOSES was chosen by God to be His special messenger to the cruel oppressor of His people. God commissioned Moses to bring his people out of bondage and slavery. But Moses wasn't sinless. He wouldn't do.

Exodus 2: 10: And the child grew, and she brought him unto Pharaoh's daughter, and he became her son. And she called his name Moses: and she said, Because I drew him out of the water.

Hebrews 11:23-26: By faith Moses, when he was born, was hid three months of his parents, because they saw he was a proper child; and they were not afraid of the king's commandment. [24] By faith Moses, when he was come to years, refused to be called the son of Pharaoh's daughter; [25] Choosing rather to suffer affliction with the people of God, than to enjoy the pleasures of sin for a season; [26] Esteeming the reproach of Christ greater riches than the treasures in Egypt.

DAVID was the king God chose to rule over His nation. He was a man after God's own heart. But he wasn't sinless. He wouldn't do.

1 Samuel 16:13: Then Samuel took the horn of oil, and anointed him in the midst of his brethren: and the Spirit of the Lord came upon David from that day forward....

Acts 13:22: And when he had removed him, he raised up unto them David to be their king; to whom also he gave testimony, and said, I have found David the son of Jesse, a man after mine own heart, which shall fulfill all my will.

DANIEL was a president under the kings of Babylon. He was a faithful man with an excellent spirit who prayed three times a day. But he wasn't sinless. He wouldn't do.

Daniel 6:1-4: It pleased Darius to set over the kingdom an hundred and twenty princes, which should be over the whole kingdom; [2] And over these three presidents; of whom Daniel was first: that the princes might give accounts unto them, and the king should have no damage. [3] Then this Daniel was preferred above the presidents and princes, because an excellent spirit was in him; and the king thought to set him over the whole realm. [4] Then the presidents and princes sought to find occasion against Daniel concerning the kingdom; but they could find none occasion nor fault; forasmuch as he was faithful, neither was there any error or fault found in him.

Nowhere among the prophets, priests, judges or kings could God find a man worthy of this task. None were without sin. None of them would do.

Romans 3:23: For all have sinned, and come short of the glory of God;

Romans 3:10-12: As it is written, There is none righteous, no, not one: [11] There is none that understandeth, there is none that seeketh after God. [12] They are all gone out of the way, they are together become unprofitable; there is none that doeth good, no, not one.

God had the Solution:

God had promised to destroy the enemy of mankind. He had given His Word. He would have to do it Himself. But God is a God of justice and honor and His Word is His bond. When God placed Adam in the garden He gave him dominion and authority over the earth. In turn Adam gave his dominion and authority over to the enemy. God no longer had a right to intervene in the affairs of men.

The only people with authority in the earth are those born on the planet. If God were to regain what Adam lost and return His creation to its original state He would have to find a way to become legal in the earth. He would have to put on flesh by being born into the world as a male child. He would have to live life as a human being and experience everything that causes men to stumble, without making a misstep. His life would have to be perfect. He would have to be not a good man but a God man.

Genesis 3:15: And I will put enmity between thee and the woman, and between thy seed and her seed; it shall bruise thy head, and thou shalt bruise his heel.

God decided to clothe His Word in flesh and send Him to dwell among men without sinning and experience death for everyone. The Word agreed to go.

John 1:1-5: In the beginning was the Word, and the Word was with God, and the Word was God. [2] The same was in the beginning with God. [3] All things were made by him; and without him was not any thing made that was made. [4] In him was life; and the life was the light of men. [5] And the light shineth in darkness; and the darkness comprehended it not.

John 1:14: And the Word was made flesh, and dwelt among us, (and we beheld his glory, the glory as of the only begotten of the Father,) full of grace and truth.

God has yet Another Problem:

How do I put flesh on my Word? In order for a man to be legal in the earth he must be born of a woman. In order for a woman to bear a child she must be impregnated with the sperm or seed of a man. Once again the search was on. This time God needed a woman willing to carry His seed – His Word. (Mark 4:3-14). She had to be a faithful believer and a virgin, meaning never having had sexual intercourse.

Isaiah 7:14: Therefore the Lord himself shall give you a sign; Behold, a virgin shall conceive, and bear a son, and shall call his name Immanuel.

Matthew 1:23: Behold, a virgin shall be with child, and shall bring forth a son, and they shall call his name Emmanuel, which being interpreted is, God with us. Mark 4:14: The sower soweth the word.

God has the Solution:

"I'll find a willing virgin."

Again God searches the annals of time:

EVE was the first woman but she had to become the "Mother of All Living". She couldn't remain a virgin. She wasn't available.

Genesis 3:20: And Adam called his wife's name Eve; because she was the mother of all living.

Lot, Abraham's nephew, was left with two VIRGIN DAUGHTERS, but they had serious trust issues. When they thought their father was the last man on earth they both got pregnant by him. God couldn't use them. They weren't eligible.

Genesis 19:36: Thus were both the daughters of Lot with child by their father.

DEBORAH was too busy advancing the cause of women by fulfilling her calling to be the only female judge of Israel. She was married but had no time for a baby. All Israel were her children. She wasn't available.

Judges 4:4-5: And Deborah, a prophetess, the wife of Lapidoth, she judged Israel at that time. [5] And she dwelt under the palm tree of Deborah between Ramah and Bethel in mount Ephraim: and the children of Israel came up to her for judgment.

RUTH was a descendant of the incestuous relationship between Lot and his older daughter. She had married into the house of King David's ancestors. And she's mentioned in the genealogy of Jesus, but she was no virgin. She wasn't eligible.

Genesis 19:37: And the firstborn bare a son, and called his name Moab: the same is the father of the Moabites unto this day.

Ruth 1:22: So Naomi returned, and Ruth the Moabitess, her daughter in law, with her, which returned out of the country of Moab: and they came to Bethlehem in the beginning of barley harvest.

Matthew 1:5-6: Salmon the father of Boaz, whose mother was Rahab, Boaz the father of Obed, whose mother was Ruth, Obed the father of Jesse, and Jesse the father of King David.

ESTHER was a young, beautiful maiden chosen by King Ahasuerus as a candidate to become his new queen. She was a virgin but God had other plans for her. He needed Esther to save His chosen nation from annihilation. She wasn't available.

Esther 4:14 For if thou altogether holdest thy peace at this time, then shall there enlargement and deliverance arise to the Jews from another place; but thou and thy father's house shall be destroyed: and who knoweth whether thou art come to the kingdom for such a time as this?

MARY was a faithful young believer engaged to be married and still a virgin. But was she believer enough to take on raising God's Son? God sends the angel Gabriel to Mary with the offer to become the mother of God's only begotten Son.

Luke 1:26-33: And in the sixth month the angel Gabriel was sent from God unto a city of Galilee, named Nazareth, [27] To a virgin espoused to a man whose name was Joseph, of the house of David; and the virgin's name was Mary. [28] And the angel came in unto her, and said, Hail, thou that art highly favoured, the Lord is with thee: blessed art thou among women. [29] And when she saw him, she was troubled at his saying, and cast in her mind what manner of salutation this should be. [30] And the angel said unto her, Fear not, Mary: for thou hast found favour with God. [31] And, behold, thou shalt conceive in thy womb, and bring forth a son, and shalt call his name Jesus. [32] He shall be great, and shall be called the Son of the Highest: and the Lord God shall give unto him the throne of his father David: [33] And he shall reign over the house of Jacob for ever; and of his kingdom there shall be no end.

Mary has a Problem:

Once Mary recovers from the shock of the unexpected visit from God's messenger she's both happy and humbled to hear God has chosen her for such a task. But she has one very important question. "How can I have a baby without being with a man"?

> *Luke 1:34: Then said Mary unto the angel, How shall this be, seeing I know not a man?*

God had the Solution:

Gabriel began to explain to Mary how God's Holy Spirit would come and overshadow her with the Word God had spoken to Eve back in the Garden of Eden. God's Words are eternal. And they work like seeds. God had spoken His promise. God's messenger brought that Word to Mary. The Holy Spirit planted that Word, spiritual sperm, into Mary when she accepted God's plan. Thus began the miracle of the virgin birth, a new thing in the earth.

> *Mark 4:14: The sower soweth the word.*

> *Jeremiah 31:22: How long wilt thou go about, O thou backsliding daughter? For the Lord hath created a new thing in the earth, a woman shall compass a man.*

Luke 1:35: And the angel answered and said unto her, The Holy Ghost shall come upon thee, and the power of the Highest shall overshadow thee: therefore also that holy thing which shall be born of thee shall be called the Son of God.

Luke 1:37-38: For with God nothing shall be impossible. [38] And Mary said, Behold the handmaid of the Lord; be it unto me according to thy word. And the angel departed from her.

Mary has Another Problem:

Mary was all but married to Joseph who was a descendant of King David. What was he going to do when she tells him she's having a baby and he's not the father but it is not by another man. Can she really expect him to believe she hasn't cheated on him?

Matthew 1:18: Now the birth of Jesus Christ was on this wise: When as his mother Mary was espoused to Joseph, before they came together, she was found with child of the Holy Ghost.

Joseph has a Problem:

Joseph knows Mary is not carrying his child. But because of his love for her and his stellar character he refused to disgrace her publicly. He decided he would privately and quietly end their relationship. But Joseph was stilled troubled in his decision.

Matthew 1:19: Then Joseph her husband, being a just man, and not willing to make her a publick example, was minded to put her away privily.

God had the Solution:

Joseph tossed and turned that night, unable to rest. God sent him the same messenger He had sent to Mary, Gabriel. The angel explains that Mary's child is truly from God and he should not be afraid or concerned about making Mary his wife. Not only has she not been unfaithful, God expects him to raise the baby as his own. Gabriel tells him to name the baby boy Jesus because his name means salvation. This child will also be known as Emanuel because God has come to live with human beings and give His life for the world. Jesus is born in Bethlehem and His star brings wise men to worship the newly born King of the Jews, the King of Kings.

Matthew 1:20-25: But while he thought on these things, behold, the angel of the Lord appeared unto him in a dream, saying, Joseph, thou son of David, fear not to take unto thee Mary thy wife: for that which is conceived in her is of the Holy Ghost. And she shall bring forth a son, and thou shalt call his name Jesus: for he shall save his people from their sins. Now all this was done, that it might be fulfilled which was spoken of the Lord by the prophet, saying, Behold, a virgin shall be with child, and shall bring forth a son, and they shall call his name Emmanuel, which being interpreted is,

God with us. Then Joseph being raised from sleep did as the angel of the Lord had bidden him, and took unto him his wife: And knew her not till she had brought forth her firstborn son: and he called his name Jesus.

King Herod has a Problem:

At the time Jesus was born in Bethlehem of Judea, King Herod was reigning in Jerusalem. Because of the bright star which appeared at the time of Jesus' birth many astronomers, scientists, philosophers and explorers had tracked this phenomenon and converged on Jerusalem. The influx of such a multitude caused King Herod to inquire as to the reason Jerusalem was suddenly overrun with tourist?

The response was a shock to King Herod. He was told these travelers had come to worship the newly born King of the Jews. "What? A new king! I'm the king," was Herod's inward response. But outwardly he asked the travelers to let him know when they locate this new king that he might also come and worship the child. But Herod's true motive was to eliminate this rival for his throne. Little did he know that this King's kingdom was not limited to Israel!

Matthew 2:1-8: Now when Jesus was born in Bethlehem of Judaea in the days of Herod the king, behold, there came wise men from the east to Jerusalem, [2] Saying, Where is he that is born King of the Jews?

for we have seen his star in the east, and are come to worship him. [3] When Herod the king had heard these things, he was troubled, and all Jerusalem with him. [4] And when he had gathered all the chief priests and scribes of the people together, he demanded of them where Christ should be born. [5] And they said unto him, In Bethlehem of Judaea: for thus it is written by the prophet, [6] And thou Bethlehem, in the land of Juda, art not the least among the princes of Juda: for out of thee shall come a Governor, that shall rule my people Israel. [7] Then Herod, when he had privily called the wise men, enquired of them diligently what time the star appeared. [8] And he sent them to Bethlehem, and said, Go and search diligently for the young child; and when ye have found him, bring me word again, that I may come and worship him also.

God Foils Herod's Scheme:

By the time the traveling worshippers locate the newly born king and his family Jesus is a toddler, almost two years old. They are no longer living in the stable, where he was born, but have moved into a house pointed out by the bright star.

The wise travelers knew not to appear before a king empty handed. So they brought gifts of gold, frankincense and myrrh. These each represented an aspect of the child's future: gold to provide for His family, (this money probably allowed Joseph to move to Nazareth and set up his carpentry business); Frankincense is the incense burnt on the altar by the priests in that day and spoke to His priestly office as mediator between God and mankind; Myrrh is a spice used in burial preparation which spoke to His sacrificial death, burial and resurrection.

Once the travelers completed their mission of worship God warns them, in a dream, not to return to Herod. They went back to their own countries a by another route.

The Angel of the Lord also appeared to Joseph, in a dream, telling him to take his family and flee to the safety of Egypt and remain there until he gets word that those who seek to destroy the child are no longer a threat. So Joseph, Mary and Jesus move to Egypt.

> *Matthew 2:9-15: When they had heard the king, they departed; and, lo, the star, which they saw in the east, went before them, till it came and stood over where the young child was. [10] When they saw the star, they rejoiced with exceeding great joy. [11] And when they were come into the house, they saw the young child with Mary his mother, and fell down, and worshipped him: and when they had opened their treasures, they presented unto him gifts; gold, and frankincense, and myrrh. [12] And being warned of God in a dream that they should not return to Herod, they departed into their own country another way. [13] And when they were departed, behold, the angel of the Lord appeareth to Joseph in a dream, saying, Arise, and take the young*

child and his mother, and flee into Egypt, and be thou there until I bring thee word: for Herod will seek the young child to destroy him. [14] When he arose, he took the young child and his mother by night, and departed into Egypt: [15] And was there until the death of Herod: that it might be fulfilled which was spoken of the Lord by the prophet, saying, Out of Egypt have I called my son.

The Wrath of King Herod:

Meanwhile back in Jerusalem Herod has been waiting for the travelers to return. He soon realizes they're not coming back, which makes him extremely angry. So angry he gives an order to kill all male children in Bethlehem and the surrounding areas who were two years old or under based on the time he determined from the travelers. This horrific act caused such mourning and weeping in Judea that there was no comfort to be found.

After Herod's death God sent word to Joseph in Egypt by Gabriel to return to Israel since those who wanted to kill Jesus were dead. But when Joseph learned Herod's son was reigning in his father's stead he was afraid to go to Judea. Again God warns him in a dream to detour to the region of Galilee where they settled in Nazareth. It had been prophesied the savior of mankind would be called a Nazarene.

Matthew 2:16-23: Then Herod, when he saw that he was mocked of the wise men, was exceeding wroth, and sent forth, and slew all the children that were in Bethlehem, and in all the coasts thereof, from two years old and under, according to the time which he had diligently enquired of the wise men. [17] Then was fulfilled that which was spoken by Jeremy the prophet, saying, [18] In Rama was there a voice heard, lamentation, and weeping, and great mourning, Rachel weeping for her children, and would not be comforted, because they are not. [19] But when Herod was dead, behold, an angel of the Lord appeareth in a dream to Joseph in Egypt, [20] Saying, Arise, and take the young child and his mother, and go into the land of Israel: for they are dead which sought the young child's life. [21] And he arose, and took the young child and his mother, and came into the land of Israel. [22] But when he heard that Archelaus did reign in Judaea in the room of his father Herod, he was afraid to go thither: notwithstanding, being warned of God in a dream, he turned aside into the parts of Galilee: [23] And he came and dwelt in a city called Nazareth: that it might be fulfilled which was spoken by the prophets, He shall be called a Nazarene.

PART II
JESUS' PROBLEMS

Jesus Grows Up in Nazareth:

Now with his family safe in Nazareth, Joseph opens a carpentry business to provide for their livelihood. As the years went by the child Jesus grew strong not just in body but also in spirit. He was full of wisdom and God's favor was upon him.

Luke 2:39-40: And when they had performed all things according to the law of the Lord, they returned into Galilee, to their own city Nazareth. [40] And the child grew, and waxed strong in spirit, filled with wisdom: and the grace of God was upon him.

Jesus' Problems:

"I must be about my Father's business."

Jesus was twelve years old when the family went down to Jerusalem to celebrate the Passover feast. This had been their tradition each year. But this year would be different. The feast of the Passover lasted seven days with much worship and fellowship. When the days of feasting were over Joseph and Mary headed back to Nazareth with the rest of the caravan.

At the end of a day's travel they looked for Jesus among their relatives and friends. Little did they know Jesus was still in Jerusalem. Unable to find their only child they returned to Jerusalem in a panic. They searched the city for three days before they finally found him in the temple listening to the teachers and asking them questions. Those who heard Him were in awe at his understanding and wisdom.

Joseph and Mary were shocked when they found Jesus. His mother wanted to know why he thought it was okay to stay behind in Jerusalem without asking anyone's permission and leaving them to suffer all the anxiety of parents whose child is missing.

Jesus' reply: "Why were you looking for me? Didn't you know I had to be about my Father's business"? Joseph had to restrain Mary from slapping Jesus across the room. As far as she was concerned his Father's business was carpentry.

Luke 2:41-50: Now his parents went to Jerusalem every year at the feast of the Passover. [42] And when he was twelve years old, they went up to Jerusalem after the custom of the feast. [43] And when they had fulfilled the days, as they returned, the child Jesus tarried behind in Jerusalem; and Joseph and his mother knew not of it. [44] But they, supposing him to have been in the company, went a day's journey; and they sought him among their kinsfolk and acquaintance. [45] And when they found him not, they turned back again to Jerusalem, seeking him. [46] And it came to pass, that after three days they found him in the temple, sitting in the midst of the doctors, both hearing them, and asking them questions. [47] And all that heard him were astonished at his understanding and answers. [48] And when they saw him, they were amazed: and his mother said unto him, Son, why hast thou thus dealt with us? behold, thy father and I have sought thee sorrowing. [49] And he said unto them, How is it that ye sought me? wist ye not that I must be about my Father's business? [50] And they understood not the saying which he spake unto them.

As they journeyed back to Nazareth Joseph reminded Mary of what happened when Jesus was eight days old and they took him to the Temple to present him to God . . . (flashback)

On that day two of God's faithful ministers, Simeon and Anna were also in the temple. They were both up in age and had been waiting for God to reveal to them the one appointed to save mankind from itself.

When Jesus' family brought him in Simeon took the baby in his arms and turned his face toward heaven and said: "Thank you Lord. I can die in peace now that my eyes have seen the savior you promised." Anna came at the same moment giving thanks to God and speaking about the child to all who were looking for the Savior, that he in deed had come.

Luke 2:34-38: And Simeon blessed them, and said unto Mary his mother, Behold, this child is set for the fall and rising again of many in Israel; and for a sign which shall be spoken against; [35] (Yea, a sword shall pierce through thy own soul also,) that the thoughts of many hearts may be revealed. [36] And there was one Anna, a prophetess, the daughter of Phanuel, of the tribe of Aser: she was of a great age, and had lived with an husband seven years from her virginity; [37] And she was a widow of about fourscore and four years, which departed not from the temple, but served God with fastings and prayers night and day. [38] And she coming in that instant gave thanks likewise unto the Lord, and spake of him to all them that looked for redemption in Jerusalem.

For the next eighteen years Mary and Joseph (until his death) pondered all these special circumstances concerning their son.

Luke 2:51-52: And he went down with them, and came to Nazareth, and was subject unto them: but his mother kept all these sayings in her heart. [52] And Jesus increased in wisdom and stature, and in favour with God and man.

"I Am the Son of God"

Jesus, being about thirty years old, went down to the river where His cousin John was baptizing the people. Jesus also went forward to be baptized. But John, recognizing Him to be God's chosen one said, "You should be the one baptizing me." Jesus told him being submerged under the water was a sign of faith in God and He needed John to baptize Him also as a sign of His faith. John consented and baptized Jesus. But when he did something amazing happened. Jesus went straight up out of the water and the Spirit of God, in the form of a dove came and rested upon Him. Then there was a voice from the heavens saying: "This is my son that I love. Listen to Him because He has pleased me." And those that were there said they heard the voice of God. Jesus contemplated these things within Himself saying, "Now it is time to be about my Father's business. I am the Son of the living God."

Luke 3:21-23: Now when all the people were baptized, it came to pass, that Jesus also being baptized, and praying, the heaven was opened, [22] And the Holy Ghost descended in a bodily shape like a dove upon him, and a voice came from heaven, which said, Thou art my beloved Son; in thee I am well pleased. [23] And Jesus himself began to be about thirty years of age, being (as was supposed) the son of Joseph . . .

The word spread quickly through all the region of the young man about whom God Himself spoke at his Baptism. He became a powerful teacher in their assemblies.

There came a day when He was in His hometown of Nazareth on the Sabbath day. He went to the temple and took His place to read. He was given the book of prophecy written by Isaiah and turned to the passage which read,

The Spirit of the Lord God is upon me; because the Lord has anointed me to preach good news unto the meek; he has sent me to bind up the brokenhearted, to proclaim liberty to the captives, and the opening of the prison to them that are bound; To proclaim the acceptable year of the Lord (Isaiah 61:1-2a).

Then He closed the book, returned it to the attendant, took His seat and said, "This day this scripture is fulfilled in your ears." The people who heard Him acknowledged He spoke well but began to say, "Isn't this Joseph, the carpenter's son"? So Jesus began to tell them how a prophet is not accepted in his own country and how they'll say to him the old adage "physician heal yourself," but they should take heed to His words.

The people became angry saying we know Him and where He comes from, who does He think he is making himself a prophet? They worked themselves into an angry mob and took Him outside the city to throw Him off a cliff. But since He was truly the Son of God He simply walked through the mob and went His way. You see, it was way too soon for Jesus to be killed. The work was about to begin.

Luke 4:15-24: And he taught in their synagogues, being glorified of all. [16] And he came to Nazareth, where he had been brought up: and, as his custom was, he went into the synagogue on the sabbath day, and stood up for to read. [17] And there was delivered unto him the book of the prophet Esaias. And when he had opened the book, he found the place where it was written, [18] The Spirit of the Lord is upon me, because he hath anointed me to preach the gospel to the poor; he hath sent me to heal the brokenhearted, to preach deliverance to the captives, and recovering of sight to the blind, to set at liberty them that are bruised, [19] To preach the acceptable year of the Lord. [20] And he closed the book, and he gave it again to the minister, and sat down. And the eyes of all them that were in the synagogue were fastened on him. [21] And he began to say unto them, This day is this scripture fulfilled in your ears. [22] And all bare him witness, and wondered at the gracious words which proceeded out of his mouth. And they said, Is not this Joseph's son? [23] And he said unto them, Ye will surely say unto me this proverb, Physician, heal thyself: whatsoever we have heard done in Capernaum, do also here in thy country. [24] And he said, Verily I say unto you, No prophet is accepted in his own country.

Jesus went out and began to gather the men who would assist Him in his work. There were twelve: two sets of brothers, Andrew and Simon Peter and James, and John who were all in the fishing business along with Phillip; Levi, who was known as Matthew the tax collector; and Bartholomew who preferred to be called Nathaniel. The rest of the crew included another James, Alpheus' son; Thomas, called the doubter; another Simon known for being extremely zealous when it came to Judaism; and Judas known as Thaddeus, and not to be confused with Judas Iscariot, Jesus' childhood friend, treasurer for the group and ultimately the betrayer.

Before Jesus announced His ministry in Nazareth and chose the twelve men who would become known as His disciples He spent forty days in the desert fasting, praying and defeating the enemy of God who had come to challenge and thwart His mission.

> *Luke 4:1-13: And Jesus being full of the Holy Ghost returned from Jordan, and was led by the Spirit into the wilderness, [2] Being forty days tempted of the devil. And in those days he did eat nothing: and when they were ended, he afterward hungered. [3] And the devil said unto him, If thou be the Son of God, command this stone that it be made bread. [4] And Jesus answered him, saying, It is written, That man shall not live by bread alone, but by every word of God. [5] And the devil, taking him up into an high mountain, shewed unto him all the kingdoms of the world in a moment of time. [6] And the devil said unto him, All this power will I give thee, and the glory of them: for that is delivered unto me; and to whomsoever I will I give it. [7] If thou therefore wilt worship me, all shall be thine. [8] And Jesus answered and said unto him, Get thee behind me, Satan: for it is written, Thou shalt worship the Lord thy God, and him only shalt thou serve. [9] And he brought him to Jerusalem, and set him on a*

pinnacle of the temple, and said unto him, If thou be the Son of God, cast thyself down from hence: [10] For it is written, He shall give his angels charge over thee, to keep thee: [11] And in their hands they shall bear thee up, lest at any time thou dash thy foot against a stone. [12] And Jesus answering said unto him, It is said, Thou shalt not tempt the Lord thy God. [13] And when the devil had ended all the temptation, he departed from him for a season.

The Ministry Years

Jesus went to Capernaum where the people were more receptive to His teaching. He spent His time there ministering to the needs of the people, performing miracles and gathering a great following.

Luke 4:31-32: And came down to Capernaum, a city of Galilee, and taught them on the sabbath days. [32] And they were astonished at his doctrine: for his word was with power.

On one occasion a woman, who had been hemorrhaging for twelve years crawled her way through the crowd in order to touch the hem of Jesus clothes. She believed and said to herself, "If I can but touch the hem of His garment I will be cured." She was right. When she touched Jesus' clothes she felt the healing power of God flow into her body. It was so strong Jesus felt it flow out of

Him and asked, "Who touched Me?" The woman told Him she had spent all her money on doctors for all those years without relief but now touching Him had made her well.

> *Luke 8:43-48: And a woman having an issue of blood twelve years, which had spent all her living upon physicians, neither could be healed of any, [44] Came behind him, and touched the border of his garment: and immediately her issue of blood stanched. [45] And Jesus said, Who touched me? When all denied, Peter and they that were with him said, Master, the multitude throng thee and press thee, and sayest thou, Who touched me? [46] And Jesus said, Somebody hath touched me: for I perceive that virtue is gone out of me. [47] And when the woman saw that she was not hid, she came trembling, and falling down before him, she declared unto him before all the people for what cause she had touched him and how she was healed immediately. [48] And he said unto her, Daughter, be of good comfort: thy faith hath made thee whole; go in peace.*

On that same occasion a local ruler's daughter, who was only twelve years old, had died. Jesus took Peter, James and John with Him to the ruler's house where He put the mourners out and raised the girl from the dead.

> *Luke 8:49-56: While he yet spake, there cometh one from the ruler of the synagogue's house, saying to him, Thy daughter is dead; trouble not the Master. [50] But when Jesus heard it, he answered him, saying, Fear not:*

believe only, and she shall be made whole. [51] And when he came into the house, he suffered no man to go in, save Peter, and James, and John, and the father and the mother of the maiden. [52] And all wept, and bewailed her: but he said, Weep not; she is not dead, but sleepeth. [53] And they laughed him to scorn, knowing that she was dead. [54] And he put them all out, and took her by the hand, and called, saying, Maid, arise. [55] And her spirit came again, and she arose straightway: and he commanded to give her meat. [56] And her parents were astonished: but he charged them that they should tell no man what was done.

On another occasion Jesus healed Peter's mother-in-law who had fallen ill; afterwards, she prepared a meal for them.

Luke 4:38-39: And he arose out of the synagogue, and entered into Simon's house. And Simon's wife's mother was taken with a great fever; and they besought him for her. [39] And he stood over her, and rebuked the fever; and it left her: and immediately she arose and ministered unto them.

The disciples spent three and a half years with Jesus going throughout Israel as He taught on the kingdom of God, preached about things to come, healed the sick, raised the dead, gave sight to the blind, restored the deaf and crippled and cast evil spirits out of those who were obsessed, depressed or possessed by them.

But Jesus also had a social side. His very first miracle was at a wedding in a little town called Cana in Galilee. He and his family had gone to the wedding and during the reception the couple ran out of wine. His mother, Mary, asked Him to intervene. Then she told the waiters to do whatever He said. Jesus simply told them to fill the water pots with water. To their amazement, when the headwaiter poured it into a carafe for tasting it was the best wine he'd ever had.

John 2:1-11: And the third day there was a marriage in Cana of Galilee; and the mother of Jesus was there: [2] And both Jesus was called, and his disciples, to the marriage. [3] And when they wanted wine, the mother of Jesus saith unto him, They have no wine. [4] Jesus saith unto her, Woman, what have I to do with thee? mine hour is not yet come. [5] His mother saith unto the servants, Whatsoever he saith unto you, do it. [6] And there were set there six waterpots of stone, after the manner of the purifying of the Jews, containing two or three firkins apiece. [7] Jesus saith unto them, Fill the waterpots with water. And they filled them up to the brim. [8] And he saith unto them, Draw out now, and bear unto the governor of the feast. And they bare it. [9] When the ruler of the feast had tasted the water that was made wine, and knew not whence it was: (but the servants which drew the water knew;) the governor of the feast called the bridegroom, [10] And saith unto him, Every man at the beginning doth set forth good wine; and when men have well drunk, then that which is worse: but thou hast kept the good wine until now.

> *[11] This beginning of miracles did Jesus in Cana of Galilee, and manifested forth his glory; and his disciples believed on him.*

Jesus went to dine at the homes of His friends and those He wouldn't necessarily call friends. And on other occasions He provided food for thousands of His followers from what would normally be considered one person's lunch.

> *Luke 9:11-17: And the people, when they knew it, followed him: and he received them, and spake unto them of the kingdom of God, and healed them that had need of healing. [12] And when the day began to wear away, then came the twelve, and said unto him, Send the multitude away, that they may go into the towns and country round about, and lodge, and get victuals: for we are here in a desert place. [13] But he said unto them, Give ye them to eat. And they said, We have no more but five loaves and two fishes; except we should go and buy meat for all this people. [14] For they were about five thousand men. And he said to his disciples, Make them sit down by fifties in a company. [15] And they did so, and made them all sit down. [16] Then he took the five loaves and the two fishes, and looking up to heaven, he blessed them, and brake, and gave to the disciples to set before the multitude. [17] And they did eat, and were all filled: and there was taken up of fragments that remained to them twelve baskets.*

Often when large crowds gathered to see Jesus do miracles He would teach them using stories about natural things they understood to explain spiritual principles. These stories are called parables and there are many recorded throughout the account of Jesus ministry (Mark 4:1-34; Luke 6:17-49).

As you can imagine, Jesus had many more detractors than followers. There came a day when some religious leaders brought to Him a woman they said had been caught in the act of adultery (having sexual intercourse with a man who was not her husband). We should note, they didn't bring the man, only her. They were not interested in the punishment due a lawbreaker but whether Jesus would go against the written law that they might build a case against Him. They reminded Him the law said she should be stoned to death.

Jesus appeared to simply ignore them when He bent down and began writing on the ground. We don't know what He was writing, but He did look up long enough to say to the woman's accusers, "Whichever one of you who has kept the whole law and never broke one of them – you throw the first stone at her," and continued writing on the ground.

One by one the men dropped their rocks and walked away. Eventually there was only Jesus and the woman. He asked her, "Where are your accusers? Has no one condemned you?" She answered, "No one Lord." Jesus said, "I don't condemn you either. Go and don't make this mistake again." Jesus, the Master of compassion and wisdom.

John 8:1-11: Jesus went unto the Mount of Olives. [2] And early in the morning he came again into the temple, and all the people came unto him; and he sat down, and taught them. [3] And the scribes and Pharisees brought unto him a woman taken in adultery; and when they had set her in the midst, [4] They say unto him, Master, this woman was taken in adultery, in the very act. [5] Now Moses in the law commanded us, that such should be stoned: but what sayest thou? [6] This they said, tempting him, that they might have to accuse him. But Jesus stooped down, and with his finger wrote on the ground, as though he heard them not. [7] So when they continued asking him, he lifted up himself, and said unto them, He that is without sin among you, let him first cast a stone at her. [8] And again he stooped down, and wrote on the ground. [9] And they which heard it, being convicted by their own conscience, went out one by one, beginning at the eldest, even unto the last: and Jesus was left alone, and the woman standing in the midst. [10] When Jesus had lifted up himself, and saw none but the woman, he said unto her, Woman, where are those thine accusers? hath no man condemned thee? [11] She said, No man, Lord. And Jesus said unto her, Neither do I condemn thee: go, and sin no more.

Jesus and his followers moved on to an area called Caesarea Philippi. There He asked His disciples this question: "Who do men say that I am?" And they replied some say you are John the Baptist (back from the dead, who was executed by a corrupt government), some say Elijah or Jeremiah or one of the other prophets of long ago. Then Jesus asked them: "But who do you say that I am?" Peter spoke up and said, "You are the Christ, the Son of the Living God." Jesus said, "Peter, you didn't get this knowledge through your natural senses. My Father God has revealed this to you. And you are blessed because of it."

Then Jesus instructed them not to tell anyone that He was The Christ, Savior, and Messiah. He began to explain to His disciples how He had to go to Jerusalem where He would be accused of treason, tried and killed by the elders, scribes and chief priests and be raised from the dead after three days. But they had no understanding, at this point, how this could ever happen.

Matthew 16:13-21: When Jesus came into the coasts of Caesarea Philippi, he asked his disciples, saying, Whom do men say that I the Son of man am? [14] And they said, Some say that thou art John the Baptist: some, Elias; and others, Jeremias, or one of the prophets. [15] He saith unto them, But whom say ye that I am? [16] And Simon Peter answered and said, Thou art the Christ, the Son of the living God. [17] And Jesus answered and said unto him, Blessed art thou, Simon Barjona: for flesh and blood hath not revealed it unto thee, but my Father which is in heaven. [18] And I say also unto thee, That thou art Peter, and upon this rock I will build my church; and the gates of hell shall not prevail against it. [19] And I will give unto thee the keys of the kingdom of heaven: and whatsoever thou shalt bind on earth shall be bound in heaven: and whatsoever thou shalt loose on earth shall be loosed in heaven. [20] Then charged he his disciples that they should tell no man that he was Jesus the Christ. [21] From that time forth began Jesus to shew unto his disciples, how that he must go unto Jerusalem, and suffer many things of the elders and chief priests and scribes, and be killed, and be raised again the third day.

About a week later, Jesus took Peter, James and John with Him up into a high mountain to pray. While they were there Jesus was transformed before their eyes. His face was shining bright as the sun and His clothes were like pure white light and glistening. There appeared with Him two men, also in white and glowing, talking with Him about His impending death, burial and resurrection. They were Moses representing God's commands and Elijah representing the prophets of God. Peter, James and John were so awestruck they actually passed out. When they came to, Peter in his excitement, suggested they build three memorial buildings: one for Jesus, one for Moses and one for Elijah. As he was speaking a bright cloud came and overshadowed them. And a voice came out of the cloud saying, "This is My beloved Son who has pleased Me well. Listen to Him."

When the disciples heard the voice they fell on

their faces in fear. Jesus touched them saying, "Get up and don't be afraid." At this point they saw only Jesus and as they came down the mountain Jesus told them not to speak of these events until after He had risen from the dead. So they kept these things between themselves and wondered what He meant about rising from the dead.

Matthew 17:1-9: And after six days Jesus taketh Peter, James, and John his brother, and bringeth them up into an high mountain apart, [2] And was transfigured before them: and his face did shine as the sun, and his raiment was white as the light. [3] And, behold, there appeared unto them Moses and Elias talking with him. [4] Then answered Peter, and said unto Jesus, Lord, it is good for us to be here: if thou wilt, let us make here three tabernacles; one for thee, and one for Moses, and one for Elias. [5] While he yet spake, behold, a bright cloud overshadowed them: and behold a voice out of the cloud, which said, This is my beloved Son, in whom I am well pleased; hear ye him. [6] And when the disciples heard it, they fell on their face, and were sore afraid. [7] And Jesus came and touched them, and said, Arise, and be not afraid. [8] And when they had lifted up their eyes, they saw no man, save Jesus only. [9] And as they came down from the mountain, Jesus charged them, saying, Tell the vision to no man, until the Son of man be risen again from the dead.

Jesus and His disciples continued to travel throughout Israel spreading the news "the

Kingdom of God is at hand" with many signs, wonders and miracles of healing the sick, giving sight to the blind, restoring the crippled and raising the dead.

As they made their way back toward Jerusalem and came to the Mount of Olives, Jesus sent two disciples ahead to the village. He instructed them to go and find a donkey that's been tied with her colt and bring them to Him. They went and found the animals and when the people there asked why they were taking them away they told them, "The Lord has need of them," as Jesus had instructed. So the let them go.

The two disciples brought the animals to Jesus and put garments on their backs so Jesus could ride on them. The crowds gathered as they always did when Jesus was around. But this time they cut branches from the palm trees and laid them in the road as Jesus rode into Jerusalem. He usually walked. But there was something different and significant about this day, as the people would soon see.

The crowds waved the palm branches in the air and surrounded Jesus as He rode shouting,

Hosanna to the Son of David. Blessed is He that comes in the Name of the Lord; Hosanna in the highest. Blessed be the King that comes in the name of the Lord: peace in heaven and glory in the highest.

Some of the religious leaders who were there told Jesus to stop the people from praising Him and hailing Him as king. They were afraid of the Roman authorities who had the rule over their nation. They didn't want to be accused of treason for having a king other than Caesar. Jesus told them if the people kept silent the very rocks on the ground would instantly begin to shout His praises.

As Jesus rode on He began to weep when He could see Jerusalem in the distance. His foreknowledge of the destruction that was to come saddened Him greatly, along with the fact they would fail to recognize their deliverer (Matt 23:37-39).

> *Matthew 21:1-9: And when they drew nigh unto Jerusalem, and were come to Bethphage, unto the mount of Olives, then sent Jesus two disciples, [2] Saying unto them, Go into the village over against you, and straightway ye shall find an ass tied, and a colt with her: loose them, and bring them unto me. [3] And if any man say ought unto you, ye shall say, The Lord hath need of them; and straightway he will send them. [4] All this was done, that it might be fulfilled which was spoken by the prophet, saying, [5] Tell ye the daughter of Sion, Behold, thy King cometh unto thee, meek, and sitting upon an ass, and a colt the foal of an ass. [6] And the disciples went, and did as Jesus*

commanded them, [7] And brought the ass, and the colt, and put on them their clothes, and they set him thereon. [8] And a very great multitude spread their garments in the way; others cut down branches from the trees, and strawed them in the way. [9] And the multitudes that went before, and that followed, cried, saying, Hosanna to the Son of David: Blessed is he that cometh in the name of the Lord; Hosanna in the highest.

Luke 19:38-41 Saying, Blessed be the King that cometh in the name of the Lord: peace in heaven, and glory in the highest. [39] And some of the Pharisees from among the multitude said unto him, Master, rebuke thy disciples. [40] And he answered and said unto them, I tell you that, if these should hold their peace, the stones would immediately cry out. [41] And when he was come near, he beheld the city, and wept over it

When Jesus got to Jerusalem He went straight to the temple. The circumstances He found there upset Him greatly. The people coming to worship were being cheated by the so-called "money changers" who were charging an unfair rate of exchange for the temple currency and compelling them to buy the lambs and doves, needed for the offering, from them. (Sound familiar?)

Jesus, driven by holy indignation, turned over the tables where they were conducting business and drove them out of the temple with a whip He made from cords (John 2:15). He would not allow anyone to carry merchandise through the temple, proclaiming, "Is it not written, My house shall be called of all nations the house of prayer? But you have made it a den of thieves!"

Mark 11:15-17: And they come to Jerusalem: and Jesus went into the temple, and began to cast out them that sold and bought in the temple, and overthrew the tables of the moneychangers, and the seats of them that sold doves; [16] And would not suffer that any man should carry any vessel through the temple. [17] And he taught, saying unto them, Is it not written, My house shall be called of all nations the house of prayer? but ye have made it a den of thieves.

This made the religious leaders angry enough to want Him dead. But, they were afraid to touch Him because of the multitudes of people who were being blessed by His miracles and teachings. So, they came up with a scheme to trap Him with His own words. They sent their henchmen to ask Him a loaded question. The men approached Jesus, calling Him "Master" on pretense. They said they knew He was a teacher sent from God to show them the way of truth. They asked whether He thought it was lawful to pay their taxes to the Roman Caesar or not? Jesus, knowing their hypocrisy, asked them to show Him the tax money. They brought Him a coin. Now, Jesus asked them whose face and inscription was on the money? They answered – Caesar's. Therefore Jesus told them to "give to Caesar the things that belong to Caesar and give God the things that belong to God." They were amazed by His answer and went away leaving Him alone - for now.

Matthew 22:15-22: Then went the Pharisees, and took counsel how they might entangle him in his talk. [16] And they sent out unto him their disciples with the Herodians, saying, Master, we know that thou art true, and teachest the way of God in truth, neither carest thou for any man: for thou regardest not the person of men. [17] Tell us therefore, What thinkest thou? Is it lawful to give tribute unto Caesar, or not? [18] But Jesus perceived their wickedness, and said, Why tempt ye me, ye hypocrites? [19] Shew me the tribute money. And they brought unto him a penny. [20] And he saith unto them, Whose is this image and superscription? [21] They say unto him, Caesar's. Then saith he unto them, Render therefore unto Caesar the things which are Caesar's; and unto God the things that are God's. [22] When they had heard these words, they marveled, and left him, and went their way.

In two days it will be time for the Passover feast. This is the same feast where Jesus stayed behind in Jerusalem while His family was on their way back to Nazareth when He was twelve years old, about twenty-one years earlier.

Jesus taught in the temple constantly and the chief priests along with the religious politicians could no longer tolerate His actions. But because of His popularity with the people they were afraid to arrest Him openly. The word went out: anyone having information on the whereabouts of and how to apprehend Jesus would be rewarded for such information.

Many of Jesus' followers expected the Messiah to lead a revolution against the foreign rule of the Romans over the Hebrew nation. But when that didn't appear to be part of Jesus' plan, there were those who attempted to force His hand. What better way to do this than to have Him arrested!

> *Matthew 26:3-4: Then assembled together the chief priests, and the scribes, and the elders of the people, unto the palace of the high priest, who was called Caiaphas, [4] And consulted that they might take Jesus by subtilty, and kill him.*

"I must lay down my life."

> *John 10:17-18: Therefore doth my Father love me, because I lay down my life, that I might take it again. [18] No man taketh it from me, but I lay it down of myself. I have power to lay it down, and I have power to take it again. This commandment have I received of my Father.*

Now the feast of the Passover was two days away and Jesus told His disciples He would be betrayed and put to death. At the same time the chief priests and the religious leaders were plotting to accomplish this very thing.

Judas Iscariot, one of the twelve who had been a childhood friend of Jesus, decided it was time to make a move. He went to the religious leaders and made a deal to turn over Jesus for thirty pieces of silver. They were glad Judas had volunteered to help them destroy Jesus.

In the meantime, Jesus was preparing to celebrate the Passover feast with His disciples for the last time. He had already instructed Peter and John where to find the place to prepare the feast.

That evening they all gathered in the large upper room of the house where the meal had been prepared. As they ate Jesus began telling them how He was going to be betrayed into the hands of His enemies by one of them. This raised cause for concern and sadness in each of their hearts and all began to question if they were the one that would do this terrible thing. Even Judas questioned "Master, is it I?" But he already knew.

Matthew 26:1-4: And it came to pass, when Jesus had finished all these sayings, he said unto his disciples, [2] Ye know that after two days is the feast of the passover, and the Son of man is betrayed to be crucified. [3] Then assembled together the chief priests, and the scribes, and the elders of the people, unto the palace of the high priest, who was called Caiaphas, [4] And consulted that they might take Jesus by subtilty, and kill him.

Psalm 41:9: Yea, mine own familiar friend, in whom I

trusted, which did eat of my bread, hath lifted up his heel against me.

Luke 22:7-13: Then came the day of unleavened bread, when the passover must be killed. [8] And he sent Peter and John, saying, Go and prepare us the passover, that we may eat. [9] And they said unto him, Where wilt thou that we prepare? [10] And he said unto them, Behold, when ye are entered into the city, there shall a man meet you, bearing a pitcher of water; follow him into the house where he entereth in. [11] And ye shall say unto the goodman of the house, The Master saith unto thee, Where is the guestchamber, where I shall eat the passover with my disciples? [12] And he shall shew you a large upper room furnished: there make ready. [13] And they went, and found as he had said unto them: and they made ready the passover.

Matthew 26:20-22: Now when the even was come, he sat down with the twelve. [21] And as they did eat, he said, Verily I say unto you, that one of you shall betray me. [22] And they were exceeding sorrowful, and began every one of them to say unto him, Lord, is it I?

Matthew 26:25: Then Judas, which betrayed him, answered and said, Master, is it I? He said unto him, Thou hast said.

Jesus told them His betrayer would be the one He gave a morsel of food as they ate from a common dish. When the time came He gave the food to Judas Iscariot and told him whatever he was about to do, do it quickly. ("No man takes my life. I lay it down.") Judas left the assembly but the other disciples were unaware of what was happening. They thought Jesus had sent him to buy something for the feast or to provide things for the poor because he was the treasurer for the group. Once Judas was gone, Jesus began to talk about the significance of this Passover meal and how it would be the last time He'd share in this feast with them until He came into His kingdom.

As they were eating Jesus took a particular loaf of bread, blessed it, broke it and gave it to them saying, "This represents my body which is given for you. Take and eat it in remembrance of me." ("No man takes my life. I lay it down.")

Then He took the cup after supper known as the cup of redemption, gave thanks to God and said, "This cup is the new covenant (agreement) written in my blood which is shed for you. Drink all of it to remove your sins. For as often as you eat this bread and drink this cup you do remember the Lord's death until He returns. ("No man takes my life. I lay it down.")

> *John 13:21-30: When Jesus had thus said, he was troubled in spirit, and testified, and said, Verily, verily, I say unto you, that one of you shall betray me. [22] Then the disciples looked one on another, doubting of whom he spake. [23] Now there was leaning on Jesus' bosom one of his disciples, whom Jesus loved. [24]*

Simon Peter therefore beckoned to him, that he should ask who it should be of whom he spake. [25] He then lying on Jesus' breast saith unto him, Lord, who is it? [26] Jesus answered, He it is, to whom I shall give a sop, when I have dipped it. And when he had dipped the sop, he gave it to Judas Iscariot, the son of Simon. [27] And after the sop Satan entered into him. Then said Jesus unto him, That thou doest, do quickly. [28] Now no man at the table knew for what intent he spake this unto him. [29] For some of them thought, because Judas had the bag, that Jesus had said unto him, Buy those things that we have need of against the feast; or, that he should give something to the poor. [30] He then having received the sop went immediately out: and it was night.

Matthew 26:26-29: And as they were eating, Jesus took bread, and blessed it, and brake it, and gave it to the disciples, and said, Take, eat; this is my body. [27] And he took the cup, and gave thanks, and gave it to them, saying, Drink ye all of it; [28] For this is my blood of the new testament, which is shed for many for the remission of sins. [29] But I say unto you, I will not drink henceforth of this fruit of the vine, until that day when I drink it new with you in my Father's kingdom

1 Cor. 11:26: For as often as ye eat this bread, and drink this cup, ye do shew the Lord's death till he come.

After dinner there was a heated discussion among the disciples as to which of them should be counted the greatest in this kingdom Jesus was about to establish. Jesus told them whomever desired greatness let them first be a servant. Then Jesus got up, wrapped a towel around Himself and began to wash their feet, illustrating what He had just explained.

Then Jesus said to them,

You call me Lord and Master (Teacher) and you're right. I am. If I'm your Lord and Master and I wash your feet you should be willing to do the same for one another. I've shown you the servant is not greater than his master. Neither is the messenger greater than the one who sent the message. If you know and understand these things it will bring you happiness to do them. I'm telling you, whoever receives who I send receives Me and whoever receives Me receives the one who sent Me.

In all this Jesus was alluding to the fact that once He was gone there would be those continuing to carry His message of love and redemption throughout the world. Those of us who believe the message and receive Him also receives the Father God who sent Him.

They ended the evening with a song and went out to the Mount of Olives. There they followed Jesus to a garden called Gethsemane where He took Peter, James and John aside with Him and went to pray. But this was no ordinary prayer meeting.

Unlike times past, this night Jesus went into deep sorrow and heaviness. The reality of what He was about to do began to set in. He was about to allow Himself to take the most horrible punishment imaginable for crimes He never committed. He was about to die for the sins (crimes against God) of a world that didn't even know who He was. His anguish was so great He literally sweat so much blood it fell to the ground where He knelt.

At one point He prayed there would be some other way to accomplish this task of saving mankind. But in the final analysis Jesus submitted His will to the will of the Father that the plan for mankind's redemption would be completed. ("No man takes my life. I lay it down.")

Luke 22:24: And there was also a strife among them, which of them should be accounted the greatest.

John 13:4-5: He riseth from supper, and laid aside his garments; and took a towel, and girded himself. [5] After that he poureth water into a bason, and began to wash the disciples' feet, and to wipe them with the towel wherewith he was girded.

John 13:13-20: Ye call me Master and Lord: and ye say well; for so I am. [14] If I then, your Lord and Master, have washed your feet; ye also ought to wash one another's feet. [15] For I have given you an example, that ye should do as I have done to you. [16] Verily, verily, I say unto you, The servant is not greater than his lord; neither he that is sent greater than he that sent him. [17] If ye know these things, happy are ye if ye do them. [18] I speak not of you all: I know whom I have chosen: but that the scripture may be fulfilled, He that eateth bread with me hath lifted up his heel against me. [19] Now I tell you before it come, that, when it is come to pass, ye may believe that I am he. [20] Verily, verily, I say unto you, He that receiveth whomsoever I send receiveth me; and he that receiveth me receiveth him that sent me.

Mark 14:26: And when they had sung an hymn, they went out into the mount of Olives.

Mark 14:32-34: And they came to a place which was named Gethsemane: and he saith to his disciples, Sit ye here, while I shall pray. [33] And he taketh with him Peter and James and John, and began to be sore amazed, and to be very heavy; [34] And saith unto them, My soul is exceeding sorrowful unto death: tarry ye here, and watch.

Luke 22:41-44: And he was withdrawn from them about a stone's cast, and kneeled down, and prayed, [42] Saying, Father, if thou be willing, remove this cup from me: nevertheless not my will, but thine, be done. [43] And there appeared an angel unto him from heaven, strengthening him. [44] And being in an agony he prayed more earnestly: and his sweat was as it were great drops of blood falling down to the ground.

The Betrayal

When Jesus finished praying He came and found His disciples sleeping. He woke them up saying the time had come, His betrayer was at hand. At that point Judas showed up with the officers sent by the religious leaders to arrest Jesus. Since it was night and they weren't sure which one was Jesus. Judas had told them to arrest the one he kissed.

Judas was able to lead the officers to the garden because he knew this was a place where Jesus often prayed. Once they found Him Judas cried "Master, Master," and kissed Him. At that point Peter drew his sword and cut off one of the men's ear. Jesus told Peter to put away his sword and reached out and healed the man's ear, still displaying nothing but love and compassion.

Jesus turned to His betrayer and said, "Judas, you betray the Son of Man with a kiss?" ("No man takes my life. I lay it down.") Jesus is arrested and the disciples flee.

> *Matthew 26:47-52, 56: And while he yet spake, lo, Judas, one of the twelve, came, and with him a great multitude with swords and staves, from the chief priests and elders of the people. [48] Now he that betrayed him gave them a sign, saying, Whomsoever I shall kiss, that same is he: hold him fast. [49] And forthwith he came to Jesus, and said, Hail, master; and kissed him. [50] And*

Jesus said unto him, Friend, wherefore art thou come? Then came they, and laid hands on Jesus, and took him. [51] And, behold, one of them which were with Jesus stretched out his hand, and drew his sword, and struck a servant of the high priest's, and smote off his ear. [52] Then said Jesus unto him, Put up again thy sword into his place: for all they that take the sword shall perish with the sword. [56] But all this was done, that the scriptures of the prophets might be fulfilled. Then all the disciples forsook him, and fled.

The Trial

That night the religious leaders formed a council to examine the claims of Jesus to find a reason to have Him executed. (You see, the Jewish rulers only had the power delegated to them by the Roman government. They were afraid Jesus would be the cause of them losing their power. The people were calling Jesus king and looking to Him to deliver them from the oppression of the Romans and those they had placed in power over them.)

Jesus is brought bound before the Jewish council and the high priest questions Him about what He's been teaching the people. Jesus told them He had spoken openly for all to hear and if he wanted to know what He said he should ask those who heard Him. Just then an officer slapped Him in the face telling Him not to talk back to the high priest. Jesus said, "If I lied prove it. Otherwise why did you hit me?" ("No man takes my life. I lay it down.")

The council tried to find witnesses to testify against Jesus. But since their accounts of His actions were not true they couldn't find two witnesses with the same story. They said they heard Him say He would destroy the temple and rebuild it in three days as if by magic.

But their accounts did not agree. So the high priest asked Him, "Are you the Savior, the Son of God?" Jesus answered, "I am. And you'll see me sitting on the right hand of the throne of God and coming in the clouds of heaven."

At this the high priest ripped his robe as a sign of outrage and said to the council, "We don't need any witnesses now. We've all heard Him speak blasphemy, putting Himself on a level equal to God."

And they all said He is guilty and condemned him to death. Then they spat on Him and blindfolded Him and began to punch him in the face asking Him which one of them hit Him, mocking and beating Him. ("No man takes my life. I lay it down.")

John 18:19-23: The high priest then asked Jesus of his disciples, and of his doctrine. [20] Jesus answered him, I spake openly to the world; I ever taught in the synagogue, and in the temple, whither the Jews always resort; and in secret have I said nothing. [21] Why askest thou me? ask them which heard me, what I have said unto them: behold, they know what I said. [22] And when he had thus spoken, one of the officers which stood by struck Jesus with the palm of his hand, saying, Answerest thou the high priest so? [23] Jesus answered him, If I have spoken evil, bear witness of the evil: but if well, why smitest thou me?

Mark 14:55-65: And the chief priests and all the council sought for witness against Jesus to put him to death; and found none. [56] For many bare false witness against him, but their witness agreed not together. [57] And there arose certain, and bare false witness against him, saying, [58] We heard him say, I will destroy this temple that is made with hands, and within three days I will build another made without hands. [59] But neither so did their witness agree together. [60] And the high priest stood up in the midst, and asked Jesus, saying, Answerest thou nothing? what is it which these witness against thee? [61] But he held his peace, and answered nothing. Again the high priest asked him, and said unto him, Art thou the Christ, the Son of the Blessed? [62] And Jesus said, I am: and ye shall see the Son of man sitting on the right hand of power, and coming in the clouds of heaven. [63] Then the high priest rent his clothes, and saith, What need we any further witnesses? [64] Ye have heard the blasphemy: what think ye? And they all condemned him to be guilty of death. [65] And some began to spit on him, and to cover his face, and to buffet him, and to say unto him, Prophesy: and the servants did strike him with the palms of their hands.

Betrayer's Remorse

The next morning the council of religious leaders bound Jesus and took Him to the governor. The council could sentence the condemned man to death, but they had no power to carry out the sentence. They had to take Jesus to the Roman appointed governor which at that time was Pontius Pilate.

When Judas saw Jesus was condemned to death he was overcome with remorse. He tried to undo the deed by taking the money back to the council and telling them he had betrayed an innocent man. They told him that was his problem and they could care less. Judas went out and hung himself!

Matthew 27:1-5: When the morning was come, all the chief priests and elders of the people took counsel against Jesus to put him to death: [2] And when they had bound him, they led him away, and delivered him to Pontius Pilate the governor. [3] Then Judas, which had betrayeth him, when he saw that he was condemned, repented himself, and brought again the thirty pieces of silver to the chief priests and elders, [4] Saying, I have sinned in that I have betrayed the innocent blood. And they said, What is that to us? see thou to that. [5] And he cast down the pieces of silver in the temple, and departed, and went and hanged himself.

Jesus before Pilate

Jesus is brought to the judgment hall of the governor and Pilate asked what the charges against this man were? They accused Him of treason saying He told the people not to pay taxes to Caesar and that He Himself was Christ a king. Pilate asked Him, "Are you the king of the Jews?" Jesus replied, "That is what you say."

Then Pilate told the crowd which had gathered he could find no cause to condemn this man. The leaders protested saying, "He came from Galilee and has gone all about the country teaching and stirring up the people."

When Pilate heard he was a Galilean he thought he had a way out. Galilee was under the jurisdiction of Herod Antipas who happened to be in Jerusalem for the festival. Pilate sent Jesus to Herod.

> *John 18:29: Pilate then went out unto them, and said, What accusation bring ye against this man?*

> *Luke 23:2-7: And they began to accuse him, saying, We found this fellow perverting the nation, and forbidding to give tribute to Caesar, saying that he himself is Christ a King. [3] And Pilate asked him, saying, Art thou the King of the Jews? And he answered him and said, Thou sayest it. [4] Then said Pilate to the chief priests and to the people, I find no fault in this man. [5]*

And they were the more fierce, saying, He stirreth up the people, teaching throughout all Jewry, beginning from Galilee to this place. [6] When Pilate heard of Galilee, he asked whether the man were a Galilean. [7] And as soon as he knew that he belonged unto Herod's jurisdiction, he sent him to Herod, who himself also was at Jerusalem at that time.

Jesus before Herod Antipas

Herod had wanted to see Jesus for sometime. He'd heard all about Him and hoped to see Him perform some great miracle. He was delighted for the chance to finally see Jesus. But his delight was soon turned to disappointment and anger. When Herod questioned Jesus he got no reply. Jesus remained silent and answered nothing nor did He "perform" any miracles. ("No man takes my life. I lay it down.")

The chief priests and leaders continued vigorously with their accusations. Herod's guards mocked Jesus putting a royal robe on Him as if He were the king. Then they took Him back to Pilate. That day the enmity between Pilate and Herod ended.

Luke 23:8-12: And when Herod saw Jesus, he was exceeding glad: for he was desirous to see him of a long season, because he had heard many things of him; and he hoped to have seen some miracle done by him. [9] Then he questioned with him in many words; but he answered him nothing. [10] And the chief priests and scribes stood and vehemently accused him. [11] And Herod with his men of war set him at nought, and mocked him, and arrayed him in a gorgeous robe, and sent him again to Pilate. [12] And the same day Pilate and Herod were made friends together: for before they were at enmity between themselves.

Jesus before Pilate the Second Time

At this festival the governor could release a prisoner of the people's choosing. Pilate could see it was jealousy, fear and hatred that motivated Jesus' accusers. He knew He had done nothing worthy of death. There was no real case against Jesus. Pilate wanted to release Him.

Now there was another notable prisoner named Barabbas who was a rebel and a murderer. The religious leaders persuaded the people to ask for Barabbas. The open forum became a shouting match between those yelling for Jesus' release and those wanting Barabbas. Pilate spoke to the crowd asking, "Who do you want me to release to you, Barabbas the murderer or Jesus who is called king?" Unfortunately, those calling for Barabbas prevailed. Pilate then asked, "What shall I do with Jesus?" The crowd screamed, "Crucify Him!" Pilate asked, "Why? What horrible crime has He committed that He should be crucified?" (You see, this was the most horrible and torturous form of execution imaginable.)

When Pilate saw there was no way of reasoning with this unruly crowd he took water and washed his hands in front of them saying, "I am innocent of the blood of this just man. You see to it." Then the people said, "Let His blood be on us and on our children." (They didn't realize what they were saying.) Then Pilate released Barabbas and delivered Jesus to the guards who beat Him mercilessly before they crucified Him. ("No man takes my life. I lay it down.")

> *Matthew 27:15-18, 20-26: Now at that feast the governor was wont to release unto the people a prisoner, whom they would. [16] And they had then a notable prisoner, called Barabbas. [17] Therefore when they were gathered together, Pilate said unto them, Whom will ye that I release unto you? Barabbas, or Jesus which is called Christ? [18] For he knew that for envy they had delivered him. [20] But the chief priests and elders persuaded the multitude that they should ask Barabbas, and destroy Jesus. [21] The governor answered and said unto them, Whether of the twain will ye that I release unto you? They said, Barabbas. [22] Pilate saith unto them, What shall I do then with Jesus which is called Christ? They all say unto him, Let him be crucified. [23] And the governor said, Why, what evil hath he done? But they cried out the more, saying, Let him be crucified. [24] When Pilate saw that he could prevail nothing, but that rather a tumult was made, he took water, and washed his hands before the multitude, saying, I am innocent of the blood of this just person: see ye to it. [25] Then answered all the*

> *people, and said, His blood be on us, and on our children. [26] Then released he Barabbas unto them: and when he had scourged Jesus, he delivered him to be crucified*

The Cruelty of the Guards

The guards took Jesus and stripped Him of His clothes and beat Him with a whip that could inflict many lashes at one strike. Each lash had bits of glass and metal imbedded and attached to them so as to dig into the skin and rip out pieces of flesh with every strike. They beat Him until He no longer looked like a man (Isa.52: 14 & 53:5).

Then they plaited a crown of thorns and pound it into His scalp. They put a purple robe on Him and said, "Hail, King of the Jews!" bowing in mock worship. They spat on Him and hit Him in the face with their fists. They brought Him back before the people wearing the purple robe and the crown of thorns. Pilate said, "Behold the Man!"

When the religious leaders saw Him they demanded He be crucified. The governor again stated he could fine no reason to execute Jesus. The Jewish rulers said their law demands Jesus be put to death because He made Himself the Son of God. When Pilate heard this he was even more afraid because his wife's earlier warning to have nothing to do with Jesus, calling Him a just man, because of an upsetting dream she had about Him.

Now Pilate took Jesus back into the judgment hall and asked Him, "Who are you?" Jesus didn't answer. "Why won't you talk to me?" he asked. "Don't you realize I have the power to release you or put you to death?" Jesus told Pilate the only power he has is what's been given to him by a higher authority and it's the ones who brought Him before Pilate who have committed the crime. ("No man takes my life. I lay it down.")

From this point on Pilate sought to release Jesus. But the Jews said, "If you let this man go you are not Caesar's friend because whoever makes himself a king speaks against Caesar." Pilate brought Jesus out and said, "Behold your king!" They answered, "We have no king but Caesar." Pilate gave up and the guards led Jesus away to be crucified. ("No man takes my life. I lay it down.")

> *John 19:1-16: Then Pilate therefore took Jesus, and scourged him. [2] And the soldiers platted a crown of thorns, and put it on his head, and they put on him a purple robe, [3] And said, Hail, King of the Jews! and they smote him with their hands. [4] Pilate therefore went forth again, and saith unto them, Behold, I bring him forth to you, that ye may know that I find no fault in him. [5] Then came Jesus forth, wearing the crown of thorns, and the purple robe. And Pilate saith unto them, Behold the man! [6] When the chief priests therefore and officers saw him, they cried out, saying, Crucify him, crucify him. Pilate saith unto them, Take ye him, and crucify him: for I find no fault in him. [7]*

The Jews answered him, We have a law, and by our law he ought to die, because he made himself the Son of God. [8] When Pilate therefore heard that saying, he was the more afraid; [9] And went again into the judgment hall, and saith unto Jesus, Whence art thou? But Jesus gave him no answer. [10] Then saith Pilate unto him, Speakest thou not unto me? knowest thou not that I have power to crucify thee, and have power to release thee? [11] Jesus answered, Thou couldest have no power at all against me, except it were given thee from above: therefore he that delivered me unto thee hath the greater sin. [12] And from thenceforth Pilate sought to release him: but the Jews cried out, saying, If thou let this man go, thou art not Caesar's friend: whosoever maketh himself a king speaketh against Caesar. [13] When Pilate therefore heard that saying, he brought Jesus forth, and sat down in the judgment seat in a place that is called the Pavement, but in the Hebrew, Gabbatha. [14] And it was the preparation of the passover, and about the sixth hour: and he saith unto the Jews, Behold your King! [15] But they cried out, Away with him, away with him, crucify him. Pilate saith unto them, Shall I crucify your King? The chief priests answered, We have no king but Caesar. [16] Then delivered he him therefore unto them to be crucified. And they took Jesus, and led him away.

Isaiah 52:14: As many were astonied at thee; his visage was so marred more than any man, and his form more than the sons of men:

> Isaiah 53:5: But he was wounded for our transgressions, he was bruised for our iniquities: the chastisement of our peace was upon him; and with his stripes we are healed.

> Mark 15:17-19: And they clothed him with purple, and platted a crown of thorns, and put it about his head, [18] And began to salute him, Hail, King of the Jews! [19] And they smote him on the head with a reed, and did spit upon him, and bowing their knees worshipped him.

The Journey to the Cross

The guards removed the purple robe and put Jesus' own clothes on Him. They led Him along a route lined with those who mocked and those who wept at the sight of Jesus so horribly wounded struggling to carry His cross. He was so weak from the beatings and loss of blood, the guards drafted a passerby to carry the cross for Him. Along the way they offered Him a concoction of drugged vinegar to dull the pain but He refused. ("No man takes my life. I lay it down.")

When they got to the hill called " The Place of the Skull" also known as Calvary, they nailed His wrists and feet to the cross and hung Him between two crucified criminals. Then the guards gambled amongst themselves for His clothes.

Mark 15:20-24: And when they had mocked him, they took off the purple from him, and put his own clothes on him, and led him out to crucify him. [21] And they compel one Simon a Cyrenian, who passed by, coming out of the country, the father of Alexander and Rufus, to bear his cross. [22] And they bring him unto the place Golgotha, which is, being interpreted, The place of a skull. [23] And they gave him to drink wine mingled with myrrh: but he received it not. [24] And when they had crucified him, they parted his garments, casting lots upon them, what every man should take.

Surely He Died on Calvary

Now Calvary, where Jesus was executed, was close to the city and many people passed by. Pilate therefore had a title written and placed above Jesus' head which read "Jesus of Nazareth – The King of the Jews." It was written in Hebrew, Greek and Latin for all to read. When the religious leaders saw the sign they protested saying, "Don't call Him the king of the Jews but write that He said 'I am king of the Jews.'" Pilate told them, "What I have written, I have written."

Jesus, in the midst of His suffering and the clamor from the crowd, lifted His voice and said, "Father forgive them. They don't know what they're doing." ("No man takes my life. I lay it down.")

Meanwhile, the guards are mockingly yelling for Him to come down from the cross and save

Himself if He is God's king. And the criminals hanging with Him are screaming for Him to save Himself and them. But Jesus spotted His mother, Mary, in the midst of the crowd, standing with John near the foot of His cross. He said to His mother, "Woman, look to your son" (John). And He said to John, "See your mother." From this point on John took Mary into his home.

Now one of the criminals hanging with Jesus realized he and the other thief were being duly punished for their deeds but Jesus had done nothing worthy of the death penalty. He asked Jesus to remember him when He came into His kingdom. Jesus told him, "Today you will be with me in Paradise." ("No man takes my life. I lay it down.")

By this time three hours had passed, but it was only noon when something strange happened. Darkness fell as though it were midnight. Jesus cried out in a loud voice, "My God, My God, why have you left me?" Those standing by said, "He's calling for help. Let's see if anyone comes to His rescue." Jesus said, "I thirst."

Up to this point Jesus had been concerned about everyone except Himself. He had ministered to the crowd by asking God to forgive their error. He had ministered to His family by giving His disciple John the guardianship of His mother. He had ministered to the one thief by granting him

forgiveness and entrance into Paradise.
When the darkness fell Jesus turned His attention to God the Father. For the first time in all eternity God the Son (The Word) was separated from God the Father. The Son of God had taken on the sin of all mankind. Sin cannot exist in the presence of a Holy God. God the Father had to remove Himself, His presence (His Spirit) from Jesus. So Jesus cried, "Why have you forsaken me?"

Knowing His Father's plan and purpose didn't lessen the pain of separation. Being alone and seeking some relief from His suffering, Jesus said, "I thirst." To quench His thirst, they gave Him vinegar on a sponge. After he drank He said, "It is finished," meaning He had accomplished His task. His last statement was "Father, into your hands I commit my spirit," and He died. ("No man takes my life. I lay it down.")

Now it was customary to break the legs of the condemned men to speed death along. You see, the crucified men died of suffocation. Their position on the tree (cross) caused them to have to rise up on their feet to lift their chest to breathe. When their legs were broken, death was soon to follow since they couldn't breath.

The guards wanted the prisoner's to hurry and die because a High Sabbath day was approaching and they couldn't handle dead bodies on Sabbath days. But when they came to Jesus to break His legs they discovered He was already dead. One of the guards stabbed Him in the side to make sure. All this was done to fulfill the prophecies, of the Messiah which said none of His bones would be broken and they would look upon Him whom they pierced.

John 19:19-27: And Pilate wrote a title, and put it on the cross. And the writing was, JESUS OF NAZARETH THE KING OF THE JEWS. [20] This title then read many of the Jews: for the place where Jesus was crucified was nigh to the city: and it was written in Hebrew, and Greek, and Latin. [21] Then said the chief priests of the Jews to Pilate, Write not, The King of the Jews; but that he said, I am King of the Jews. [22] Pilate answered, What I have written I have written. [23] Then the soldiers, when they had crucified Jesus, took his garments, and made four parts, to every soldier a part; and also his coat: now the coat was without seam, woven from the top throughout. [24] They said therefore among themselves, Let us not rend it, but cast lots for it, whose it shall be: that the scripture might be fulfilled, which saith, They parted my raiment among them, and for my vesture they did cast lots. These things therefore the soldiers did. [25] Now there stood by the cross of Jesus his mother, and his mother's sister, Mary the wife of Cleophas, and Mary Magdalene. [26] When Jesus therefore saw his mother, and the disciple standing by, whom he loved, he saith unto his mother, Woman, behold thy son! [27] Then saith he to the disciple, Behold thy mother! And from that hour that disciple took her unto his own home.

Luke 23:33-43: And when they were come to the place, which is called Calvary, there they crucified him, and the malefactors, one on the right hand, and the other on the left. [34] Then said Jesus, Father, forgive them; for they know not what they do. And they parted his raiment, and cast lots. [35] And the people stood beholding. And the rulers also with them derided him, saying, He saved others; let him save himself, if he be Christ, the chosen of God. [36] And the soldiers also mocked him, coming to him, and offering him vinegar, [37] And saying, If thou be the king of the Jews, save thyself. [38] And a superscription also was written over him in letters of Greek, and Latin, and Hebrew, THIS IS THE KING OF THE JEWS. [39] And one of the malefactors which were hanged railed on him, saying, If thou be Christ, save thyself and us. [40] But the other answering rebuked him, saying, Dost not thou fear God, seeing thou art in the same condemnation? [41] And we indeed justly; for we receive the due reward of our deeds: but this man hath done nothing amiss. [42] And he said unto Jesus, Lord, remember me when thou comest into thy kingdom. [43] And Jesus said unto him, Verily I say unto thee, To day shalt thou be with me in paradise.

Mark 15:33-36: And when the sixth hour was come, there was darkness over the whole land until the ninth hour. [34] And at the ninth hour Jesus cried with a loud voice, saying, Eloi, Eloi, lama sabachthani? which is, being interpreted, My God, my God, why hast thou forsaken me? [35] And some of them that stood by, when they heard it, said, Behold, he calleth Elias. [36] And one ran and filled a spunge full of vinegar, and put it on a reed, and gave him to drink, saying, Let alone; let us see whether Elias will come to take him down.

John 19:28-30: After this, Jesus knowing that all things were now accomplished, that the scripture might be fulfilled, saith, I thirst. [29] Now there was set a vessel full of vinegar: and they filled a sponge with vinegar, and put it upon hyssop, and put it to his mouth. [30] When Jesus therefore had received the vinegar, he said, It is finished: and he bowed his head, and gave up the ghost.

Luke 23:44-46: And it was about the sixth hour, and there was a darkness over all the earth until the ninth hour. [45] And the sun was darkened, and the veil of the temple was rent in the midst. [46] And when Jesus had cried with a loud voice, he said, Father, into thy hands I commend my spirit: and having said thus, he gave up the ghost.

John 19:31-37: The Jews therefore, because it was the preparation, that the bodies should not remain upon the cross on the sabbath day, (for that sabbath day was an high day,) besought Pilate that their legs might be broken, and that they might be taken away. [32] Then came the soldiers, and brake the legs of the first, and of the other which was crucified with him. [33] But when they came to Jesus, and saw that he was dead already, they brake not his legs: [34] But one of the soldiers with a spear pierced his side, and forthwith came there out blood and water. [35] And he that saw it bare record, and his record is true: and he knoweth that he saith true, that ye might believe. [36] For these things were done, that the scripture should be fulfilled, A bone of him shall not be broken. [37] And again another scripture saith, They shall look on him whom they pierced.

Beyond Death

When Jesus died the earth responded. There were great earthquakes and when the ground opened many believers got up out of their graves, went into Jerusalem and were seen by the people. Then one of the guards who witnessed these strange events, struck with fear exclaimed, "Truly this was the Son of God!"

Matthew 27:51-54 the earth did quake, and the rocks rent; [52] And the graves were opened; and many bodies of the saints which slept arose, [53] And came out of the graves after his resurrection, and went into the holy city, and appeared unto many. [54] Now when the centurion, and they that were with him, watching Jesus, saw the earthquake, and those things that were done, they feared greatly, saying, Truly this was the Son of God.

The Burial

That evening one of the religious leaders, who was a disciple, came to Pilate and asked to have the body of Jesus released to him. Pilate was surprised Jesus was already dead and let him have the body. Joseph of Arimathea, that was his name, took Jesus and wrapped Him in linen and laid Him in his own new tomb. This tomb was in a nearby garden and was carved in the rock. The women who followed Jesus, Mary Magdalene and the others were also there. The plan was to return after the Sabbath day to properly prepare the body with the spices and ointments that were traditionally used. A large stone was used to close the tomb and they departed.

Matthew 27:57-61: When the even was come, there came a rich man of Arimathaea, named Joseph, who also himself was Jesus' disciple: [58] He went to Pilate, and begged the body of Jesus. Then Pilate commanded the body to be delivered. [59] And when Joseph had taken the body, he wrapped it in a clean linen cloth, [60] And laid it in his own new tomb, which he had hewn out in the rock: and he rolled a great stone to the door of the sepulchre, and departed. [61] And there was Mary Magdalene, and the other Mary, sitting over against the sepulchre.

Mark 15:44: And Pilate marveled if he were already dead: and calling unto him the centurion, he asked him whether he had been any while dead.

John 19:41-42: Now in the place where he was crucified there was a garden; and in the garden a new sepulchre, wherein was never man yet laid. [42] There laid they

Jesus therefore because of the Jews' preparation day; for the sepulchre was nigh at hand.
Luke 23:56: And they returned, and prepared spices and ointments; and rested the sabbath day according to the commandment.

The Next Day

The next day Pilate ordered the tomb to be sealed and guards stationed at the grave. The religious leaders wanted to be sure no one tampered with the grave. They reminded Pilate Jesus had promised to rise from the dead after three days. They said, His disciples might try to steal the body and say He rose from the dead. So, they set a watch to make it as secure as they could.

Matthew 27:62-66: Now the next day, that followed the day of the preparation, the chief priests and Pharisees came together unto Pilate, [63] Saying, Sir, we remember that that deceiver said, while he was yet alive, After three days I will rise again. [64] Command therefore that the sepulchre be made sure until the third day, lest his disciples come by night, and steal him away, and say unto the people, He is risen from the dead: so the last error shall be worse than the first. [65] Pilate said unto them, Ye have a watch: go your way, make it as sure as ye can. [66] So they went, and made the sepulchre sure, sealing the stone, and setting a watch.

Resurrection

When the Sabbath was over Mary Magdalene, Mary (the mother of James), Jo Anna, Salome and the other women came with their spices to anoint Jesus' body. They wondered how they'd get into the tomb because of the stone over the entrance. Suddenly there was another earthquake. But this one was caused by angels, who came down from heaven and rolled the stone away. They appeared at the door of the tomb in glistening white garments. The guards were so afraid they passed out cold, as though they were dead.

Mark 16:1: And when the sabbath was past, Mary Magdalene, and Mary the mother of James, and Salome, had bought sweet spices, that they might come and anoint him.

Matthew 28:2-4: And, behold, there was a great earthquake: for the angel of the Lord descended from heaven, and came and rolled back the stone from the door, and sat upon it. [3] His countenance was like lightning, and his raiment white as snow: [4] And for fear of him the keepers did shake, and became as dead men.

Luke 24:10: It was Mary Magdalene, and Joanna, and Mary the mother of James, and other women that were with them, which told these things unto the apostles.

The Angels' Message

"Why do you look for the living among the dead?" the angels asked the women. "You're looking for Jesus of Nazareth who was crucified. He is not here. He is risen. Come see the place where they laid Him. And go and tell His disciples to meet Him in Galilee. They will see Him there as He said."

The others went back to tell the disciples what they had seen and what the angels said. But, Mary Magdalene stayed by the tomb. The disciples didn't believe the women and thought they were hysterical with fear. But Peter and John went to the tomb to check their story. Mary Magdalene met them saying someone had taken the Lord's body and they didn't know where it was taken. John and Peter went inside the tomb and found the linen clothes lying where Jesus had been. But the cloth that covered His head was folded neatly by itself.

Matthew 28:5-8: And the angel answered and said unto the women, Fear not ye: for I know that ye seek Jesus, which was crucified. [6] He is not here: for he is risen, as he said. Come, see the place where the Lord lay. [7] And go quickly, and tell his disciples that he is risen from the dead; and, behold, he goeth before you into Galilee; there shall ye see him: lo, I have told you. [8] And they departed quickly from the sepulchre with fear and great joy; and did run to bring his disciples word.

Mark 16:6-8: And he saith unto them, Be not affrighted: Ye seek Jesus of Nazareth, which was crucified: he is risen; he is not here: behold the place where they laid him. [7] But go your way, tell his disciples and Peter that he goeth before you into Galilee: there shall ye see him, as he said unto you. [8] And they went out quickly, and fled from the sepulchre; for they trembled and were amazed: neither said they any thing to any man; for they were afraid.

Luke 24:11-12: And their words seemed to them as idle tales, and they believed them not. [12] Then arose Peter, and ran unto the sepulchre; and stooping down, he beheld the linen clothes laid by themselves, and departed, wondering in himself at that which was come to pass.

Christ Appears

Mary Magdalene remained outside the garden tomb crying. When she looked inside she saw the two angels sitting where Jesus body had been. They asked her why she was crying. She said, "They have taken away my Lord and I don't know where they have laid Him." At that point she turned and saw a man she thought must be the gardener. He asked her why she cried. Her reply was the same except she asked him if he were the one who moved the body. And if so, where had he taken it that she might retrieve and tend to the Lord's body. Jesus said, "Mary." It was not he gardener! Mary gasped, "Master!" and reached out to touch Him. But Jesus told her "Don't touch me yet. I must go present myself to My Father and your Father, to My God and your God now that My task and His plan are complete. You will see me again." Now Mary Magdalene went to the disciples with great joy proclaiming she had seen the Lord!

John 20:11-18: But Mary stood without at the sepulchre weeping: and as she wept, she stooped down, and looked into the sepulchre, [12] And seeth two angels in white sitting, the one at the head, and the other at the feet, where the body of Jesus had lain. [13] And they say unto her, Woman, why weepest thou? She saith unto them, Because they have taken away my Lord, and I know not where they have laid him. [14] And when she had thus said, she turned herself back, and saw Jesus standing, and knew not that it was Jesus. [15] Jesus saith unto her, Woman, why weepest thou? whom seekest thou? She, supposing him to be the gardener saith unto him, Sir, if thou have borne him hence, tell me where thou hast laid him, and I will take him away. [16] Jesus saith unto her, Mary. She turned herself, and saith unto him, Rabboni; which is to say, Master. [17] Jesus saith unto her, Touch me not; for I am not yet ascended to my Father: but go to my brethren, and say unto them, I ascend unto my Father, and your Father; and to my God, and your God. [18] Mary Magdalene came and told the disciples that she had seen the Lord, and that he had spoken these things unto her.

Jesus also appeared to the other women who, when they saw Him, fell at His feet and worshipped Him. Two other followers saw Him as they journeyed along a certain road. But, they didn't recognize Him until they shared a meal together. When these events were reported to His disciples, they still didn't believe Jesus was alive.

In the meantime, the Jewish rulers conspired with the guards to cover up the fact that Jesus got up from the grave. They paid them to say the disciples stole the body while they slept. And this saying is commonly reported among the Jews even today.

Matthew 28:9-10: And as they went to tell his disciples, behold, Jesus met them, saying, All hail. And they came and held him by the feet, and worshipped him. [10] Then said Jesus unto them, Be not afraid: go tell my brethren that they go into Galilee, and there shall they see me.

Luke 24:13-16: And, behold, two of them went that same day to a village called Emmaus, which was from Jerusalem about threescore furlongs. [14] And they talked together of all these things which had happened. [15] And it came to pass, that, while they communed together and reasoned, Jesus himself drew near, and went with them. [16] But their eyes were holden that they should not know him.

Luke 24:33-35: And they rose up the same hour, and

returned to Jerusalem, and found the eleven gathered together, and them that were with them, [34] Saying, The Lord is risen indeed, and hath appeared to Simon. [35] And they told what things were done in the way, and how he was known of them in breaking of bread.

Matthew 28:10-15: Then said Jesus unto them, Be not afraid: go tell my brethren that they go into Galilee, and there shall they see me. [11] Now when they were going, behold, some of the watch came into the city, and shewed unto the chief priests all the things that were done. [12] And when they were assembled with the elders, and had taken counsel, they gave large money unto the soldiers, [13] Saying, Say ye, His disciples came by night, and stole him away while we slept. [14] And if this come to the governor's ears, we will persuade him, and secure you. [15] So they took the money, and did as they were taught: and this saying is commonly reported among the Jews until this day.

Jesus Appears to His Disciples

Jesus' disciples were gathered together discussing the reports of His resurrection when He appeared in the midst of them. They were terrified thinking they were seeing a ghost. Jesus showed them the scars in His hands and feet and had them touch Him so they would know He was flesh and bone and not a ghost. He even ate food with them to prove He was truly alive and well. But Thomas wasn't there. And when they told him the Lord had been there, Thomas said, he would not believe until he could see and touch Jesus for himself.

One evening, eight days later, they were all present and the doors were locked for the night. Jesus again appeared in the midst of them. He greeted them with peace and invited Thomas to inspect His hands and feet and touch the wound in His side saying, "Have some faith and stop doubting." Thomas began to worship the Lord saying, "My lord and my God!" Jesus said, "Thomas, you believe because you have seen me. But, blessed are they that have not seen and yet believe."

After these things Jesus showed Himself to His disciples, for the third time, on the Sea of Tiberias. Peter and the other disciples, who were in the fishing trade, went out fishing. They fished, all night, and caught not one single fish. That morning they saw Jesus standing on the shore but they didn't know it was He. He asked them, "Did you catch any fish?" They said no. He told them to cast the net on the right side of the ship and they'll fine fish. They did what He said and the net could hardly hold all the fish they caught. John realized it was Jesus and told Peter, "It's the Lord."

The disciples came ashore dragging the net filled with 153 huge fish. They saw a campfire with fish and bread cooked on it. Jesus invited them to "Come and dine." Again He shared a meal with

His disciples after being raised from the dead. ("No man takes my life. I lay it down. And I have the power to take it up again.")

Luke 24:36-43: And as they thus spake, Jesus himself stood in the midst of them, and saith unto them, Peace be unto you. [37] But they were terrified and affrighted, and supposed that they had seen a spirit. [38] And he said unto them, Why are ye troubled? and why do thoughts arise in your hearts? [39] Behold my hands and my feet, that it is I myself: handle me, and see; for a spirit hath not flesh and bones, as ye see me have. [40] And when he had thus spoken, he shewed them his hands and his feet. [41] And while they yet believed not for joy, and wondered, he said unto them, Have ye here any meat? [42] And they gave him a piece of a broiled fish, and of an honeycomb. [43] And he took it, and did eat before them.

John 20:24-25: But Thomas, one of the twelve, called Didymus, was not with them when Jesus came. [25] The other disciples therefore said unto him, We have seen the Lord. But he said unto them, Except I shall see in his hands the print of the nails, and put my finger into the print of the nails, and thrust my hand into his side, I will not believe.

John 21:1-4: After these things Jesus shewed himself again to the disciples at the sea of Tiberias; and on this wise shewed he himself. [2] There were together Simon Peter, and Thomas called Didymus, and Nathanael of Cana in Galilee, and the sons of Zebedee, and two other of his disciples. [3] Simon Peter saith unto them, I go a fishing. They say unto him, We also go with thee. They went forth, and entered into a ship immediately; and that night they caught nothing. [4] But when the morning was now come, Jesus stood on the shore: but the disciples knew not that it was Jesus.

John 10:17-18: Therefore doth my Father love me, because I lay down my life, that I might take it again. [18] No man taketh it from me, but I lay it down of myself. I have power to lay it down, and I have power to take it again. This commandment have I received of my Father.

The Eleven Commissioned

Jesus had told His disciples to meet Him at a familiar place of prayer on a mountain in Galilee. When they saw Him, They worshipped but some still had doubts. Jesus explained, "All power is given to me in heaven and in earth. You go and teach all the people and baptize them in the name of the Father, The Son and the Holy Spirit. Teaching them to understand and do all that I have commanded you and know I am with you always, even to the end of the ages."

Matthew 28:16-20: Then the eleven disciples went away into Galilee, into a mountain where Jesus had appointed them. [17] And when they saw him, they worshipped him: but some doubted. [18] And Jesus came and spake unto them, saying, All power is given unto me in heaven and in earth. [19] Go ye therefore, and teach all nations, baptizing them in the name of the Father, and of the Son, and of the Holy Ghost: [20] Teaching them to observe all things whatsoever I have commanded you: and, lo, I am with you alway, even unto the end of the world. Amen.

The General Commission

In the forty days Jesus was alive on the earth after His death He was seen by more than 500 people including His brother James. He didn't forget His family.

At an assembly in Jerusalem Jesus spoke about how John the Baptist had baptized them with water. But they should wait in Jerusalem to be baptized in the Holy Ghost as God the Father had promised. They wanted to know if this would be when Jesus would establish His kingdom in the earth. He told them, it was not for them to know the times and seasons that were known only to God the Father. He said the power of the Holy Ghost would enable them to be true witnesses for Him not only at home, in Jerusalem and its surrounding areas but to the farthest reaches of the earth.

Acts 1:3-8: To whom also he shewed himself alive after his passion by many infallible proofs, being seen of them forty days, and speaking of the things pertaining to the kingdom of God: [4] And, being assembled together with them, commanded them that they should not depart from Jerusalem, but wait for the promise of the Father, which, saith he, ye have heard of me. [5] For John truly baptized with water; but ye shall be baptized with the Holy Ghost not many days hence. [6] When they therefore were come together, they asked of him, saying, Lord, wilt thou at this time restore again the kingdom to Israel? [7] And he said unto them, It is not for you to know the times or the seasons, which the Father hath put in his own power. [8] But ye shall receive power, after that the Holy Ghost is come upon you: and ye shall be witnesses unto me both in Jerusalem, and in all Judaea, and in Samaria, and unto the uttermost part of the earth.

1 Cor. 15:6-7: After that, he was seen of above five hundred brethren at once; of whom the greater part remains unto this present, but some are fallen asleep. [7] After that, he was seen of James; then of all the apostles.

His Assent into Heaven

After that, Jesus led them to Bethany where He raised His hands and spoke blessings over them. As he spoke, they watched as He was taken up in a cloud toward heaven until He was out of sight. As the people stood awestruck looking at the sky two angels in white garments appeared. They wanted to know why they were standing there staring into space. The angels said, "This same Jesus you saw go up into heaven will return again in the same way He left."

So they returned to Jerusalem worshipping Jesus with great joy. They were in the temple praising and blessing God. And they went out and preached everywhere the things the Lord had taught them. And the Word of the Lord was confirmed by the miracles, signs and wonders that accompanied the teaching.

Jesus now sits at the right hand of the throne of God in heaven. And there are many other things Jesus did that are not written here. But if it were possible to write everything Jesus did I doubt the world could hold the volumes that would be written. But these things are written that you would believe that Jesus is the Son of God, the Savior of all mankind, and that believing you would have life (eternal) through His Name.

Luke 24:50-53: And he led them out as far as to Bethany, and he lifted up his hands, and blessed them. [51] And it came to pass, while he blessed them, he was parted from them, and carried up into heaven. [52] And they worshipped him, and returned to Jerusalem with great joy: [53] And were continually in the temple, praising and blessing God. Amen.

Acts 1:9-11: And when he had spoken these things, while they beheld, he was taken up; and a cloud received him out of their sight. [10] And while they looked steadfastly toward heaven as he went up, behold, two men stood by them in white apparel; [11] Which also said, Ye men of Galilee, why stand ye gazing up into heaven? this same Jesus, which is taken up from you into heaven, shall so come in like manner as ye have seen him go into heaven.

Mark 16:19: So then after the Lord had spoken unto them, he was received up into heaven, and sat on the right hand of God.

John 21:25: And there are also many other things which Jesus did, the which, if they should be written every one, I suppose that even the world itself could not contain the books that should be written. Amen.

John 20:31: But these are written, that ye might believe that Jesus is the Christ, the Son of God; and that believing ye might have life through his name.

Now there's one last problem to solve. Please keep reading.

Part III
God's Final Problem

Getting men and women everywhere to believe the love (I John 4:16).

The question is how to get you to believe God. To believe the love He has for you. God didn't send His Son into this world to condemn you or convict you or to pass sentence on you for the way you've lived your life. God sent His only Son into this messed up world to show you a better way of life. He loves you so much He wants to see you happy, healthy and prosperous in every area of your life. The only way to abundant life and eternal life is through His Son, Jesus Christ.

"How can I convince you to believe me? What else can I do?
I created you a world.
I gave you the rule over it.
I forgave you when you turned your back on me.
I showed you mercy when you lied about me.
I sent you my Son and you killed Him.
I gave you my Word and you would not believe.
I gave you great ideas and inventions and you still ignored me.
I gave you my love and you rejected me.

But still I give, I supply, I sustain your world and you continue to live your life because I love you. I have great and wonderful plans for you. I keep hoping, one day you'll believe the love I have for you, and you'll let me into your life. My only desire is that you spend eternity with me after a long and prosperous life on the earth I've given you. Only you have the solution to my final problem. Won't you solve it for me today?"

Now is the acceptable time, now is the day of salvation. You are the solution!

If you're ready to solve God's final problem just say this prayer:

Lord Jesus, I believe you are the Son of God who died for my sins and rose from the dead that I might have eternal life. Forgive me and come into my heart and be my savior. Thank you Jesus. Amen.

The following verses now belong to you. Accept them in faith.

1 John 4:16: And we have known and believed the love that God hath to us. God is love; and he that dwelleth in love dwelleth in God, and God in him.

John 3:16-18: For God so loved the world, that he gave his only begotten Son, that whosoever believeth in him should not perish, but have everlasting life. [17] For God sent not his Son into the world to condemn the world; but that the world through him might be saved. [18] He that believeth on him is not condemned: but he that believeth not is condemned already, because he hath not believed in the name of the only begotten Son of God.

John 10:10: The thief cometh not, but for to steal, and to kill, and to destroy: I am come that they might have life, and that they might have it more abundantly.

3 John 1:2: Beloved, I wish above all things that thou mayest prosper and be in health, even as thy soul prospereth.

Romans 3:23: For all have sinned, and come short of the glory of God;

Romans 6:23: For the wages of sin is death; but the gift of God is eternal life through Jesus Christ our Lord.

Romans 10:9-10: That if thou shalt confess with thy mouth the Lord Jesus, and shalt believe in thine heart that God hath raised him from the dead, thou shalt be saved. [10] For with the heart man believeth unto righteousness; and with the mouth confession is made unto salvation.

ABOUT THE AUTHOR

Charlene is a gifted teacher of the gospel that clearly and effectively breaks open the scriptures so that all ages are able to understand and grow spiritually. From her work with the "Older Boys and Girls Conference" of Chicago to her studies at the Chicago School of Ministries and her travels abroad in Israel, Europe, China, the Philippines and many other island nations she brings a wealth of wisdom and practical experience to her lessons.

She gave her life to Christ at the age of 14 and lives a life of commitment, integrity and service. The pillars of her life and ministry are instructions the Lord put into heart, "be diligent and obedient, consistently constant, relax and trust with patient continuance". Through her teaching she imparts principals that help people become stable in their relationship with the Lord and with others. Charlene has served as a choir member, Sunday school teacher, Sunday school superintendent, director of teacher training and new member orientation. She is currently a member of the pastoral staff of New Bethel Church under the leadership of Pastor Donald C. Luster. Charlene was licensed and ordained a minister of the gospel of Jesus the Christ by the late Pastor James E. Watson in 1990.

God's Problem

CHARLENE J. JOHNSON